Phyllis
Know thy Frerg

www.ShedBensonRadio.com
602.780.6918
KKNT 960 AM
Shea Benson

SHARIA-ISM IS HERE

THE BATTLE TO CONTROL WOMEN - AND EVERYONE ELSE

Joy Brighton

1

The information in this book is publicly sourced. For complete list of references and additional resources visit our website at:

Disclaimer

Acknowledgement

Congresswoman Sue Myrick
Congressmen Paul Broun, Trent Franks, Louis Gohmert, Peter King, John Shadegg, Frank Wolf
Senator Jon Kyl

For truly representing the interests of all Americans by standing up and asking the hard questions.

Women and Civil Rights Activists across America

Who remind our American leaders each day of the words of our U.S. Constitution and of their obligation as our U.S. representatives to protect our First Amendment Rights of free speech, press, religion, and equal rights and liberties for all Americans. As Joy, I am honored to know so many of you, as colleagues and dear friends.

Table of Contents

Chapter Summaries at end of each chapter

Table of Contents

Chapter Summaries at end of each chapter

Sharia-ism is Here. The Battle to Control Women – And Everyone Else.

You are holding in your hands a chronicle of the surprising inroads that Shariah, the guiding principles of Radical Islam, has made in America during the critical years of 2008-2013.

Radical Islam, also known as Political or Shariah Islam, has expanded onto every continent, and with it Sharia-ism, the political movement of Radical Islam, whose goal of totalitarian control of every nation and people is incompatible with Western values of individual liberties and inalienable rights. Sharia-ism is about politics, not religion.

Sharia-ism is about total control, not simply destruction or terrorism.

Sharia-ism, like Communism, Nazism, and Fascism before it, is propelled by leaders who govern absolutely by shutting down freedom of speech, religion, and equal justice before the law.

Why has Sharia-ism successfully rooted itself in America, while other totalitarian movements failed to become a serious threat in the United States?

A deadly super-fuel of political correctness, financial promise, partisan self-interest, and refusal to separate religion from politics, is driving Sharia-ism. It is no secret that Middle East petro-dollars are controlled by "bad actors" such as Saudi and Iranian governments and radical groups. Yet, these oil dollars are buying influence, quiet accommodation and goodwill from American Elites despite the known misalignment of these Mid-East players with America's strategic interests.

In this resource book, you will learn how uninformed United States leaders in our justice, prison and intelligence departments, politicians, corporate executives and college presidents, are enabling Sharia-ism in America.

You will also read that European and Canadian governments are doing a quick reversal of their earlier Shariah tolerance. For the past two years, debate about Sharia-ism in these regions has been fierce, and in its wake, laws are rapidly being passed to curb Shariah advances. For example:

1. Norway has banned the construction of Saudi-funded mosques (2011).
2. Switzerland has banned the construction of Mosque minarets (2009).
3. Belgium, France, Germany, Italy, Quebec & Sweden have outlawed the burqa and face veil, symbolic of Sharia-ism & legal inequality of women.
4. Ontario has banned Shariah Courts. Great Britain is trying to dismantle its Shariah Tribunal system.
5. Austria, Belgium, Cyprus, Denmark, Germany, Malta, Norway have criminalized forced marriage.
6. Proposed legislation in the U.K. to ban Shariah Islamic Law because it does not provide the same human rights, civil rights and women's rights as British Law.

Introduction

To pre-empt legal action against Sharia-ism in America, Shariah leaders have launched an attack on free political speech in America. The ability to shut down free speech and debate is necessary for the success of any totalitarian movement. In this book you will learn of the intimidation and silencing of Americans who criticize or merely question the legitimacy of the Shariah platform. This means that Americans are already living under and controlled by the most powerful Shariah Law, the Shariah Blasphemy Law.

Think about this: Today, Americans passionately and loudly debate issues of importance, such as the U.S. Debt ceiling, Gay Marriage, and Universal Health Care.

But not so for the issue of Shariah. For example, in 2012, the House Intelligence Committee denied an investigation into the possible infiltration of the Muslim Brotherhood (MB) into our U.S. Government, and scolded the five Congressmen who did not "exercise caution" in making these requests. The White House was silent. What is the fear of having "too much information" on a matter of national security?

Rep. Langevin, (D-RI), member of the Permanent Homeland Security Committee since 2005, called for the "withdrawal" or dismissal of these requests, stating:

> "Given our access to sensitive information, I also believe members of the Intelligence Committee have a special responsibility to exercise caution in making statements about national security concerns. The only reasonable action would be for the authors of these letters to take would be to withdraw their requests". Aug. 2012.

As we "exercise caution," the White House backed the Muslim Brotherhood party in Egypt, which was overthrown by civil revolution ten months later and legally banned from Egypt in Sept 2013. What do the Egyptian people know that we don't?

As we "exercise caution,"three (3) of the Jihadists involved in the September 2013 Kenya Mall massacre were young men recruited right out of their Arizona, Illinois, Maine, Minnesota and Missouri hometowns. There is reason for alarm is in America. And voices must be raised.

As we "exercise caution," girls and women in America are suffering under Sharia-ism: 30 - 40% experience abuse, thousands forced into marriage , and a growing percentage wear the full face veil or burqa. The Imam of Drancy, France, calls the niqab "a prison for women, a tool of sexist domination, incompatible with life in society".

That's why I've compiled these crucially important news stories from 2008-2013 into a single, easy-to-read "Show N' Tell" book with publicly sourced research or quotes by 75 experts, insiders, authors, elected politicians, journalists, professionals, and world leaders to provide facts, context & credibility. The significance of each news story looked at individually may be of little concern. When examined as a collective whole, disturbing patterns are hard to deny.

Joy Brighton

Joy Brighton

Special Acknowledgement to these Contributing Experts, Researchers and Reporters:

Ahmed, Qanta - *In the Land of Invisible Women*

al-Suwaij, Zainab -Founder of American Islamic Congress

Ali, Aayan Hirsi - *Nomad, The Infidel*

American Public Policy Alliance

Anderson, Carol Taber - Founder Family Security Matters

Ashraf, Ramelah - Voice of the Copts

Aslanian, Sasha - Minnesota Public Radio Reporter

Aylami, Ali - Director: Center for Democracy and Human Rights in
    Saudi Arabia

Benson, Lisa - National Security Speaker, 960 The Patriot Show

Aznar, Jose Maria - Former Spanish Prime Minister

Baumann, Jeff

Bella, Hamouda - *Radical Islam's Rules:*
    The Worldwide Spread of Extreme Sharia Law.

Benson, Lisa - nationalsecurityspeaker.com

Berends, M.G. - *Radical Islam's Rules:*
    The Worldwide Spread of Extreme Sharia Law.

Bihi, Abdirizak - American - Somali Civil Rights Community Leader

Bjorklund - Jan-Sweden Education Minister

Blair, Tony Blair - U.K. Prime Minister

Bloomberg, Michael - Mayor, New York City

Bostom, Andrew - The Legacy of Jihad

Bregman, JoAnne - Activist

Brim, Christine - Director Center for Security Policy

Burlingame, Debra - Founder 9-11 families

Cameron, David - British Prime Minister

Clapper, James - U.S. National Inteligence Director

Claudia Rossett: Foundation for the Defense of Democracies

Chesler, Dr. Phyllis - *An American Bride in Kabul*

Cochran, Andrew - The 7th Amendment Advocate

Congressman Louie Gohmert (TX)

Congressman Lynn Westmoreland (GA)

Congresswoman Michele Bachmann (MN)

Congressman Trent Franks (AZ)

Congressman Peter King (NY)

Congressman Tom Rooney (FL)

Congressman Keith Ellison (MN)

Congressman Jim Langevin (RI)

Congresswoman Sue Myrick (SC) - Former

Costello, Peter (1996-07) - Australian Treasurer

Coughlin Stephen - Major, *Team B Report*

Cox, British MP Baroness

Darwish, Nonie - *Cruel and Usual Punishment:*
    The Terrifying Global Implications of Islamic Law

Davies, Philip - U.K. Member of Parliament

Dorminey, Elizabeth - *The Federalist Society. Veiled Meaning:*
    Tolerance and Prohibition of the Hijab in the
    U.S. and France.

Donner, Piet Hein - Dutch Interior Minister

Dowd-Galley, Jonathan

Special Acknowledgement to these Contributing Experts, Researchers and Reporters:

Dunlap, Charles - Major General Charles

Ehrenfeld, Dr. Rachel - *Funding Evil*

Emerson, Steve - Founder Investigative Project on Terrorism, *American Jihad*

Ervin, Manda - Founder of Alliance of Iranian Women

Fatek, Tarek - *Chasing a Mirage: The Tragic Illusion of an Islamic State*

Feoktistov, Ilya: Director of Research, Americans for Peace & Tolerance

Fitzpatrick, Jim - MP

Forte, David - Professor of Law Cleveland State University

Frietdrich, Peter - German Interior Minister Hans

Gabreille, Brigitte - *They Must Be Stopped: Why We Must Defeat Radical Islam and How We Can Do*

Gaffney, Frank - *The Team B Report*

Gaubatz, Dave - *Muslim Mafia*

Geller, Pamela - *Freedom or Submission: On the Dangers of Islamic Extremism & American Complacency*

Goldstein, Brooke M. - The Lawfare Project

Governor Sam Brownback (KS)

Governor Bobby Jindal (LA)

Governor Jan Brewer (AZ)

Governor Bill Haslam (TN)

Gueant, Claude (2011-12) - French Interior Minister

Guondola, John - Former FBI agent

Holton, Chris - Center for Security Policy

Horowitz, David - *Radicals: Portraits of a Destructive Passion*

Howard, John - Australian Prime Minister (1996-07)

Ihsanoglu, OIC Secretary General E.

Imani, Amil- Operation Persian Gulf

Jacobs, Dr. Charles- Americans for Peace & Tolerance

Jamil, Shaykh Amer

Jasser, Dr. Zuhdi - American Islamic Center for Democracy

Khan, Farzana - President Muslim Canadian Congress

Kaplan, Lee - investigative journalist.

Kar, Mehrangiz - *Radical Islam's Rules: The Worldwide Spread of Extreme Sharia Law.*

Kataria, Narain - Founder Indian American Intellectuals Forum

Kaufman, Joe - Founder of CAIR-watch

Kedar, Mordechai - Scholar of Arabic and Islam

Khan, Dr. Muqtedar

Kumar, Vijay - Hindu Activist

Lafferty, Andrea - Director Traditional Values Coalition

Lappen, Alyssa - Investigative journalist on Middle East and Islam

Lewis, Bernard - *The Crisis of Islam*

Lopez, Claire - Middle East Intelligence Expert

Lugo, Karen J. - Podcast on Shariah Law & Conflict with Basic Individual Rights

Mahmud, Hasan Dr. - The Sharia Conundrum Film

Marshall, Paul - *Silenced: How Apostasy and Blasphemy Codes are Choking Freedom Worldwide*

Marshall, Paul - *Radical Islam's Rules: The Worldwide Spread of Extreme Sharia Law.*

McCarthy, Andrew - *Willful Blindness*

Special Acknowledgement to these Contributing Experts, Researchers and Reporters:

McGuinty, Dalton - Ontario Premier

Merkel, Angela - German Chancellor

Mowbray, Joel - investigative journalist

Muise, Robert - Senior Counsel American Freedom Law Center

Mueller, Robert - FBI Director

Mullis, Steve

Murdock, Deroy - Scripps Howard New Service Columnist

Namazie, Maryam - co-founder One Law for All

Nammi, Dianna - Iranian and Kurdish Rights Organization

Niaz, Robina - Turning Point for Women and Families

Nomani, Asra - *Standing Alone: An American Woman's Struggle for the Soul of Islam*

Phares, Walid - *The Coming Revolution: The Struggle for Freedom in the Middle East*

Phillips, Melanie - *The World Turned Upside Down; Londonistan*

Pipes, Dr. Daniel - *Militant Islam Reaches America*

Poole, Patrick - PJMedia National Security Commentator

Price, Valerie: Founder ACT Canada

Raza, Raheel- Muslims Facing Tomorrow

Saltamartini, Barbara - VP Italian Freedom People Party

Sarkozy, Nicholas - French President (2007-12)

Savage, Michael - The Savage Nation Radio Show

Schwartz, Stephen - Director of Islam & Democracy

Shea, Nina - *Persecuted: The Global Assault on Christians*

Sookdeo, Dr. Patrick - Director Institute for the Study of Islam and Christianity

Spencer, Robert Arab Winter Comes to America: The Truth About the War We're In, 2014

Spero, Rabbi Areyah - *Push Back*

Sperry, Paul - *Muslim Mafia*

Stakelback, Eric - *The Brotherhood: America's Next Great Enemy*

Stør, Jonas Gahr - Norwegian Minister of Health

Stella, Paul - *American Free Thinker Columnist*

Steyn, Mark - *American Alone*

Sultan, Wafa - *A God Who Hates*

Tabor, Carol - President Family Security Matters

Taylor, Alyson Rowan - Co-founder of StopShariahNow

Volokh, Eugene - UCLA School of Law, Free Speech

Warner, Dr. Bill - *Shariah Law for Non-Muslims*

Warraq, Ibn - Founder of Institute for Secularization of Islamic Society

Waters, Anne Marie - Co-founder One Law for All

Watson, D.C.

West, Diana - *American Betrayal: The Secret Assault on our Nation's Character*

Yerushalmi, David - Senior Counsel American Freedom Law Center

Yuen, Laura - Minnesota Public News Reporter

Zumwalt, LT. Colonel James G. - USMC

This course incorporates the combined efforts of dozens of content contributors, from the U.S., Europe, and Canada . Their work is attributed individually throughout this course.

Research, Development & Design Team

Lisa Benson, Sidney Turner, Brette Goldstein, Alyson Rowan Taylor, and Jen Davis

Chapter 1

What is Sharia-ism and Shariah Islamic Law?

Sharia-ism

insight box

Twelve years after September 11th, the Boston Marathon Bombers devastated American families on Patriot's Day, April 15, 2013. And still American leaders don't know what glue holds these radicals together?

The glue is not religion, not faith, and not terrorism.

The glue is Shariah Law. The glue is control. The glue is politics.

Shariah law is the written legal system of Radical Islam. It is the manifesto of a global anti-freedom movement called Sharia-ism. Sharia-ism is slowly eliminating individual liberties, to control global politics.

A bit like Fascism, a bit like Soviet Communism, a bit like Nazism, and a bit like South African Apartheid. Except Sharia-ism is here, in America. Now.

Christians, Jews, Muslims, Hindus, Seikhs, Buddhists, Coptics, Agnostics, and Atheists are being encouraged, intimidated, persuaded, bribed or terrorized into surrendering their individual liberties, bit by bit to the growing force of Sharia-ism. Shiite and Sunni radicals are murdering neighbors of their own sect in their quest for control.

French, German, British, Norwegian, and Canadian governments have figured this out in the past 4 years. They have publicly denounced Shariah Law as contrary to their laws, way of life, and human values. It may surprise you to know that these governments are passing laws to stop the spread of Sharia-ism. (Chapter 11) In 2013, Egyptians took to the streets to oust the leaders of Sharia-ism: the Muslim Brotherhood and their President Morsi.

Why are American leaders in government, community, education, business, religion, law and national security uneducated about Sharia-ism?

Saudi Wahhabism is "the most radical, the most violent, the most extreme and fanatical version of Islam."

By Bernard Lewis,
Foremost western scholar of Islam.

insight box

Between 1975 and 1987, the Saudis admit to having spent $48 billion or $4 billion per year on "overseas development aid," a figure which by the end of 2002 grew to over $70 billion (281 billion Saudi rials). A large but undocumented portion of this "Development aid" is to foster the spread of Wahhabism. The $1 billion per year spent by the Soviet Union Propaganda Machine during the Cold War pales in comparison with this contribution.

Testimony at Alex Alexiev in front of the U.S. Senate Subcommittee on Terrorism, Technology and Homeland Security
Thursday, June 26, 2003

insight
box

Where **Shariah** Law is enforced, U.S. Constitutional Law is violated.
Shariah Islamic "Law" is simply the written rules of Radical Islam.

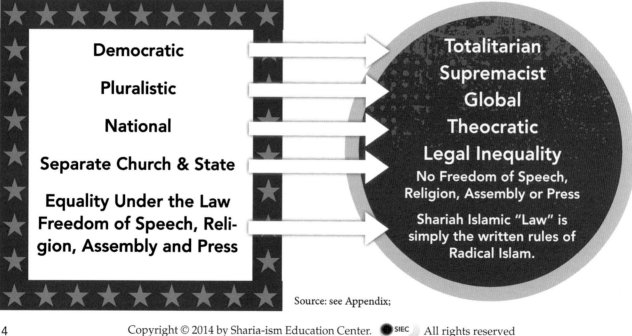

U.S. Law

Shariah Islamic Law

Democratic

Pluralistic

National

Separate Church & State

Equality Under the Law
Freedom of Speech, Reli-
gion, Assembly and Press

Totalitarian
Supremacist
Global
Theocratic
Legal Inequality
No Freedom of Speech,
Religion, Assembly or Press

Shariah Islamic "Law" is
simply the written rules of
Radical Islam.

Source: see Appendix;

insight box — U.S. law protects individual rights and freedoms. Shariah Islamic law limits individual rights and freedoms. Shariah Islamic law is nearly diametrically opposed with the U.S. Constitution.

U.S. Law

Shariah Islamic Law

U.S. Law	Shariah Islamic Law
Freedom of Religion	Infidels = submit/die
Freedom from religion	Apostasy = death
Equal Rights	Male supremacy
Murder = criminal offense	'Honor killing' forgiven
Child Marriage illegal	Child marriage permitted
Homosexuality legal	Homosexuality - death penalty
Polygamy illegal	Polygamy legal
Vigilante justice illegal	Vigilante justice sanctioned
Trial by jury & Due Process	Shariah Judges rule: No Trial by Jury or due process

insight box   Read chapter 14 to learn that in the absence of federal action, state governors are passing laws to insure that State Constitutional Law prevails over any foreign law (such as Shariah Law) which denies individual U.S. Constitutional rights of defendant.

U.S. Constitution vs. *Shariah Islamic Law*

Article Six, Section 2:
Supremacy Clause

"This Constitution, and the Laws of the United States which shall be made in Pursuance thereof; and all Treaties made, or which shall be made, under the Authority of the United States, shall be the supreme Law of the Land; and the Judges in every State shall be bound thereby, any Thing in the Constitution or Laws of any State to the Contrary notwithstanding."

Supreme

INCOMPATIBLE WITH CONSTITUTION

INCOMPATIBLE WITH CONSTITUTION

to all law

insight box

Shariah Law denies free political speech. Any criticism, by Muslims or non-Muslims, of The Prophet or any aspect of Islam is punishable by death. The European riots over the Prophet Muhammad cartoons are one example.

First Amendment   vs.   *Sharia-ism*

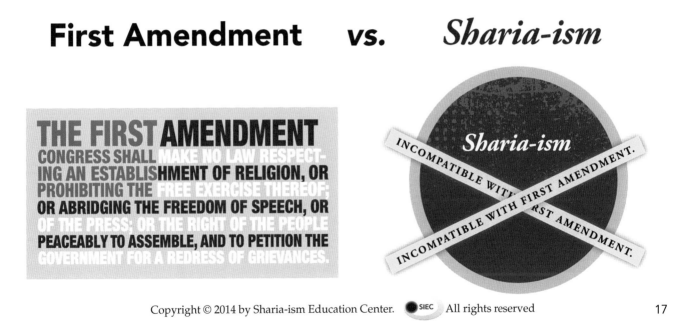

THE FIRST AMENDMENT
CONGRESS SHALL MAKE NO LAW RESPECTING AN ESTABLISHMENT OF RELIGION, OR PROHIBITING THE FREE EXERCISE THEREOF; OR ABRIDGING THE FREEDOM OF SPEECH, OR OF THE PRESS: OR THE RIGHT OF THE PEOPLE PEACEABLY TO ASSEMBLE, AND TO PETITION THE GOVERNMENT FOR A REDRESS OF GRIEVANCES.

Sharia-ism
INCOMPATIBLE WITH FIRST AMENDMENT.
INCOMPATIBLE WITH FIRST AMENDMENT.

The Qur'an is considered the divine word of Allah.

≠

The Shariah Law book is a continually evolving set of rules, written by mortal men, known as "Shariah Scholars" who seek political power and control.

According to Mohammed, the Qur'an is the immutable word of Allah as communicated to the Angel Gabriel and as recited by Mohammed (610-632AD). The Qur'an cannot be modified or supplemented.

The 1994 edition of Reliance of the Traveller is the Authoritative Rulebook of Shariah Islamic Law endorsed by the governments of Saudi Arabia, Syria, and Jordan and the al-Azhar University of Cairo.

The biographies of the 391 Shariah Scholars who have contributed to this body of work from the year 69 to the present are included. One acknowledged author is Sheikh Qaradawi; Taliban "negotiator," author and creator of fatwa to kill American soldiers and civilians overseas, creator of 53 Shariah Charity network The Union of Good designated as funder of terror by U.S. TSY. He is banned from entering the U.K. and U.S.A.

insight box

The first Shariah rules were created hundreds of years after The Prophet Mohammad's death in 7 A.D. by self-appointed leaders who sought to establish power and control over the followers of the Prophet. They accomplished this by politicizing and radicalizing Islamic thought.

Unlike the Qur'an, The Book of Shariah Laws grows over time. Shariah Scholars "derive" new laws to maintain control over evolving populations and innovation.

For example, recent Shariah rules (fatwas) forbid listening or dancing to music "corrupted by western values." Only a Shariah Scholar can decide exactly what music this is.

insight box

As the number of Governments, regions and regimes that practice Shariah Law grows, the goals and characteristics of the Sharia-ism become indisputable.

Victims of Sharia-ism are primarily:
1. Muslim women & girls
2. Non-conforming Muslims
3. Non-Muslims who refuse to convert to Sharia-ism (known as infidels or kafir)

Iran

al-Qaeda

Saudi Arabia, Iraq, Libya

Hamas: Gaza Strip in Israel

Hezbollah: Lebanon, & cells in Venezuela, Cuba, Mexico, Brazil, Paraguay

Taliban: areas of Afghanistan, Pakistan, Nigeria, Albania

Parts of Egypt, Libya, Nigeria, Pakistan, Indonesia, Sudan, Bosnia, Mali, Indonesia, Syria,

 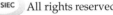

insight box

Ayatollah Khomeini installed Shariah Islamic Rule in Iran in 1979 and reversed the 65 years of modernization, economic growth, and support for women's rights, human rights, and individual rights that existed during the pre-1979 rule by Shah Pahlavi Dynasty.

Iran 1925-1979

❖ Monarchy-secular law Separation of Mosque and State.

❖ Established Women Rights: Access to higher education, careers, and right to vote. Veil is abolished. Western dress norm. Education for girls is important.

❖ Modernization of Iran: infrastructure, railroads, public education, judiciary and improved health care.

❖ Western banking.

❖ Individual Rights.

❖ Relatively Free Speech, Religion, Assembly and Press.

Islamic Republic of Iran 1979- present

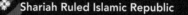

❖ Shariah Ruled Islamic Republic

❖ Theocracy: Mosque & State are one.

❖ Male Supremacy: retraction of all women's rights established under Shah.

❖ Imperialist: nuclear threat, funder of Global terrorism.

❖ No Freedom of Speech, Religion, Assembly and Press

❖ Frail economy

❖ Shariah Banking installed. Western banking illegal.

Sharia-ism seeks total world control

The political movement of Radical Islam is *Sharia-ism*. The Manifesto of Sharia-ism is a set of Shariah rules created to control Muslims and non-Muslims worldwide. The founding principles are the supremacy of Arab men over all other men (Islamic Arab Supremacy), and the supremacy of men over women (Islamic Gender Apartheid). The rules of Shariah Islamic Law mandate and create **1)** a ruling Shariah Islamist class, **2)** a submissive global class, **3)** rule over foreign states (Imperial Caliphate), **4)** women and girls as property of men, **5)** elimination of individual rights.

Chapter 2

Where Sharia-ism Lives in our World Today

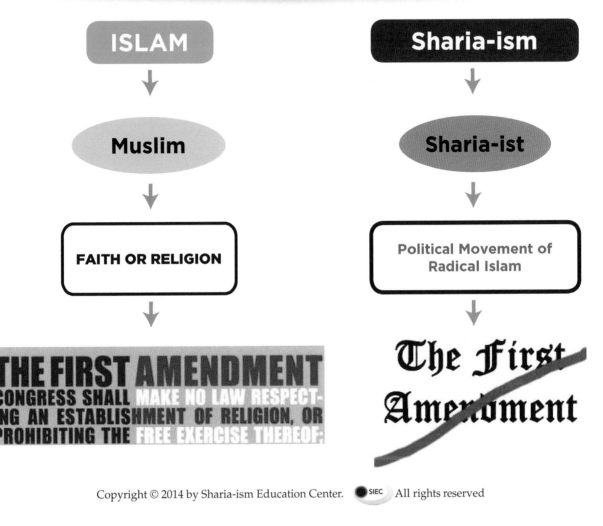

insight box

The red sphere represents the nucleus of groups which drive the global movement Sharia-ism. They gain power by controlling individual rights of all people. These "Sharia-ists" use oil wealth to buy loyalty, intimidate or terrorize. As Sharia-ism control grows, this red circle enlarges, and bleeds into the lives of all mankind (symbolized by the blue oval).

Global Community Muslims & Non-Muslims

Sharia-ism

Iran, Saudi Government,
Regions of Asian, Mid-East, and Africa

Taliban, Hamas Hezbollah
AL-Qaeda, Muslim Brotherhood

Org of Islamic Conferences (OIC)

Muslim Brotherhood Groups:
CAIR, ISNA, MPAC, ICNA

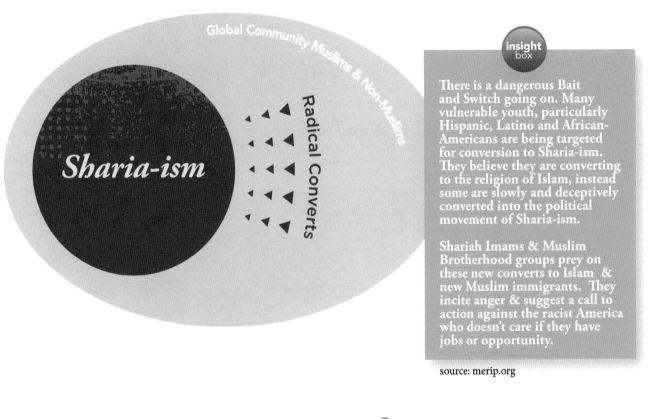

Global Community Muslims & Non-Muslims

Sharia-ism

Radical Converts

insight box

There is a dangerous Bait and Switch going on. Many vulnerable youth, particularly Hispanic, Latino and African-Americans are being targeted for conversion to Sharia-ism. They believe they are converting to the religion of Islam, instead some are slowly and deceptively converted into the political movement of Sharia-ism.

Shariah Imams & Muslim Brotherhood groups prey on these new converts to Islam & new Muslim immigrants. They incite anger & suggest a call to action against the racist America who doesn't care if they have jobs or opportunity.

source: merip.org

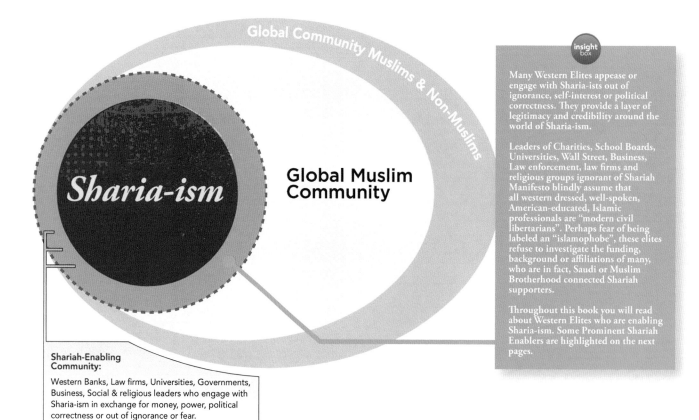

Sharia-ism

Global Muscle Community

Global Community Muslims & Non-Muslims

Global Muslim Community

Shariah-Enabling Community:

Western Banks, Law firms, Universities, Governments, Business, Social & religious leaders who engage with Sharia-ism in exchange for money, power, political correctness or out of ignorance or fear.

insight box

Many Western Elites appease or engage with Sharia-ists out of ignorance, self-interest or political correctness. They provide a layer of legitimacy and credibility around the world of Sharia-ism.

Leaders of Charities, School Boards, Universities, Wall Street, Business, Law enforcement, law firms and religious groups ignorant of Shariah Manifesto blindly assume that all western dressed, well-spoken, American-educated, Islamic professionals are "modern civil libertarians". Perhaps fear of being labeled an "islamophobe", these elites refuse to investigate the funding, background or affiliations of many, who are in fact, Saudi or Muslim Brotherhood connected Shariah supporters.

Throughout this book you will read about Western Elites who are enabling Sharia-ism. Some Prominent Shariah Enablers are highlighted on the next pages.

"In January 2013, Al Jazeera bought its way into the country by acquiring Current TV, the channel co-founded by former Vice President Al Gore, for an estimated $500 million."

"In many parts of the world Al Jazeera, owned by the emir of Qatar, is already a force to be reckoned with. But in the United States it has very little viewership because cable and satellite companies have, for the most part, declined to carry its channels."

Despite comments to the contrary, by Dec 2013, both Comcast and Time Warner Cable agreed to carry Aljazeera America Channel.

New York Times online. April 2013
USA Today, Jan 2013
Aljazeera America, 2014

While Al-Jazeera English does water down the anti-Semitic and pro-Jihad programming available on Al-Jazeera Arabic, the channels are owned by the same autocrat, the Emir of Qatar. And the "work" the channel has been doing in countries like Egypt mostly consists of provoking and covering riots and demonstrations. At the same time, the channel played down the role of the demonstrators in assaulting CBS News reporter Lara Logan, who suffered serious injuries.

New York Times online.April 2013
Huffington Post, July 2013

"We said in January that we would consider Al Jazeera America. Now that the channel is live, we think that it would be of value to our customers and are pleased to make it available,"
Melinda Witmar, Exec. VP, TIme Warner Cable

 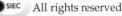

Shariah Enabler: April 2011: Huffington Post & Columbia University & Hillary Clinton back anti-American Al-Jazeera News Channel

The Al-Jazeera channel is funded by the regime in Qatar and has developed a reputation over the years as a mouthpiece for terrorist organizations such as al-Qaeda, Hamas, and Hezbollah.

Hillary Clinton

"the first partnership between Al Jazeera English and a university in the United States," Nicholas Lemann, Dean of the Columbia Journalism School, said that the journalism fellows will work in the Al-Jazeera English newsroom for 12 weeks, reporting directly to senior members of the news and programming departments. They apparently will be paid by the same regime that finances Al-Jazeera itself."

aim.org
April 2011

"Viewership of Al Jazeera is going up in the United States because it's "real news, around the clock instead of a million commercials..."
The channel, she said, was "changing peoples' minds and attitudes. And like it or hate it, it is really effective."

Secretary of State Hillary Clinton
April 2011

HuffingtonPost.com July 2013

insight box

In 2013, five years after making a 2008 "sell-out" deal with the government of Abu Dhabi, John Sexton is being criticized for his NYU 2031 plan to acquire six million additional square feet of property in Greenwich village, his university policy to boycott Israel, and his hefty $1,476,625 salary. Why isn't anyone talking about John Sexton's source of funding?

The Zakat money received by NYU was intended to "soften or reconcile the hearts of leaders", as described below. Has John Sexton accepted a gift or a bribe?

NEW YORK UNIVERSITY

2008: "NYU president John Sexton has been promised a blank check to duplicate his university on a desert island in Abu Dhabi. The expansion will leave both campuses flush with petrodollars. But to many faculty, the deal amounts to a sellout."

- New York Magazine 2008

NYU 2031 Plan:
WRONG
for NYC
WRONG
for the Village
WRONG
for NYU

villagevoice.com

Zakat: Those Whose Hearts are to be Reconciled.

"Those to be reconciled include: (1) The chief personages [political leaders] of a people (O: with weak Islamic intentions) whose Islam may be expected to improve, or whose peers may be expected to enter Islam [*da'wa*]."

1994 updated edition,
Reliance of the Traveller

(Ch. h8.14, p. 270-71)
Reliance of the Traveller

Shariah Islam

Global Community Muslims & Non-Muslims

Muslim Community
(generally born into Islam)

Revisionist/ Reformists

Secular

Modern

Liberal

Apostates

Atheists

Agnostics

insight box

These Muslims, generally born into Islam, practice the faith of Islam in their own personal, cultural, or religious way. They oppose *Shariah* fundamentalism. They are targeted as "infidels" by *Sharia-ists*

These Muslims born into Islam have chosen to reject the faith of Islam totally. Apostates choose to convert to another religion. Atheists and Agnostics reject the notion of a supreme being or the concept of faith completely. They all continue to be targeted for death by *Sharia-ists.*

Promoters of Individual Rights

Tewfik Allal
Ali Alyami & Center for Democracy
and Human Rights in Saudi Arabia.
Dr. Qanta Ahmed
Zeyno Baran
Dr. Suliman Bashear
Abdirizak Bihi
British Muslims
for Secular Democracy
Mahmoud Hassan
Center for Islamic Pluralism.
Tarek Fatah
Farid Ghadry &
Reform Party of Syria
Dr. Tawfik Hamid
Jamal Hasan
Tarek Heggy
Dr. M. Zuhdi Jasser &
American Islamic
Forum for Democracy.
Sheikh Muhammed Hisham
Sayed Parwiz Kambakhsh.
Nibras Kazimi
Naser Khader &
The Association
of Democratic Muslims.

Mufti Muhammedgali Khuzin
Shiraz Maher
Hasan Mahmud
Sanam Malik
Irshad Manji
Ahmed Subhy Mansour
Salim Mansur
Maajid Nawaz
Asra Q. Nomani
Sheikh Prof. Abdul Hadi Palazzi
Arifur Rahman
Raheel Raza
Sohail Raza
Imad Sa'ad
Maryum Samad
Secular Islam Summit
Mohamed Sifaoui
Mahmoud Mohamed Taha
Amir Taheri
Ghows Zalmay
Supna Zaidi
Muslim World Today
Council for Democracy and Tolerance
Zainab Suwaijj

insight box

These Muslim individuals or groups describe themselves as modern, liberal, secular, reformist, libertarian, or revisionist, and are labeled Civil Libertarians in this book. Most have death fatwas on their heads from Sharia-ists.

They risk their lives to educate Americans and the world of the reality of the political movement of Sharia-ism and how it differs from their faith of Islam.

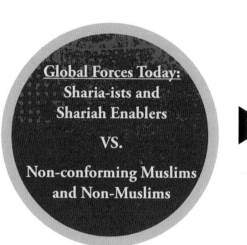

Global Forces Today:
Sharia-ists and
Shariah Enablers

VS.

Non-conforming Muslims
and Non-Muslims

1) *Sharia-ism* is the global anti-freedom movement of Radical Islam funded by, Mid-East oil dollars. The more precise term of "Sharia-ism" is replacing the vague, confusing term of "Islam-ism" by many experts.

2) Ayatollah Khomeini came to power in 1979 and converted the entire country to 100% Shariah rule, against the will of many citizens. Today when you hear "*Shariah*," think "Iran."

3) *Shariah* Enablers: Elite influencers in business, government, faith, or the community who support *Sharia-ists* instead of Muslim Civil Libertarians for any combination of these reasons: ignorance, petro-dollar profiteering, self-interest, or political correctness. American-born *Shariah* enablers in Local, State

4) and Federal government are the most powerful engine driving *Sharia-ism* in America today.

Anyone born into the faith of Islam but refuses to join the political movement of *Sharia-ism* is targeted for death as an "infidel". This includes practicing Muslims, converts (apostates), atheists and agnostics.

5) Vulnerable youth in America and other Western countries are being deceptively targeted for conversion to *Sharia-ism* Most believe they are converting to the religion of Islam.

Chapter 3

Sharia-ism Compared to other Political Movements

Islamism and Totalitarianism
Jeffrey M. Bale.
Monterey Terrorism Research and Education Program and Graduate
School of International Policy Studies

Sharia-ists want to control America.
Terrorists want to destroy America.

In March 2014, the new U.S. Council of Muslim Organizations (USCMO) was announced. Devout Muslim Dr. Zuhdi Jasser stated:

"...The USCMO "should be looked at as a circling of the wagons of the inner core of American Islamist organizations...If they were going to start an American Islamist political party those would be the founders. Instead they deceive Americans as an innocent 'Muslim coalition...

The long term goal of Sharia-ists in American is not to destroy but rather to dominate American culture, policy and law. Many Sharia-ists in America are educated in Ivy League American universities and are well-spoken business, public policy, professors, and community leaders. They value America and denounce terrorism and destruction. They simply believe that <u>their</u> way of life should be <u>our</u> way of life.

The strategy of Sharia-ists in America is to democratically build support for a Muslim Brotherhood or Sharia-ist political party. Nazism, and Soviet Communism rose to power through democratically elected parties.

Answer: Political, Mass Movement

Why?

There is not one religion in the world that mandates death for those who convert away, or imposes mortal consequences for non-believers.

- Christianity has laws exclusive to Christians.
- Buddhism has teachings exclusive to Buddhists.
- Judaism has laws exclusive to Jews.
- Confucianism has teachings exclusive to Confucianists.
- Hinduism has teachings exclusive to Hindus
- Sikhism has teachings exclusive to Sikhs

Sharia-ism has laws for Muslims and non-Muslims. These laws call for the death penalty for those who convert away from Islam or will not submit to *Sharia-ism. Sharia-ism* is a political movement, not a religion.

insight box

"Religions make demands on believers."

"Political movements make demands or require special accommodations of believers **and** non-believers."

- Dr. Bill Warner, author of *Shariah for Non-Muslims*

 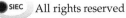

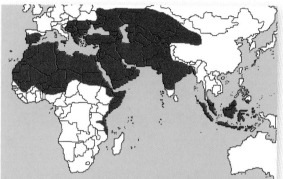

Areas at one time under Muslim rule

"The Prime Minister of Turkey, Mustafa Ataturk emerged from WWI as a national hero by abolishing the Ottoman Caliphate and Shariah laws on March 3, 1924."

- answers.com

Islamic Male Supremacism:

The belief that Islam is superior to other religions, cultures, and governmental systems, and the belief that Muslim men alone carry this mantle of superiority which entitles them to dominate, control, and rule women, non-conforming Muslims and non-Muslims.

Caliphate:

The goal of reuniting Muslims under a single flag (Caliphate) stands at the heart of the radical Islamic ideology. When Osama bin Laden called the Sept. 11 attacks on the World Trade Center and the Pentagon "a very small thing compared to this humiliation and contempt for more than 80 years," the reference was to the aftermath of World War I, when the Caliphate was abolished. "The Voice of the Caliphate." is the name of the Al-Qaeda newscast launched in 2005.

Karl Vick, Washington Post, 2006

Parallels: *Sharia-ism* and Chinese Maoism

insight box Totalitarian political movements like Sharia-ism & Chinese Maoism , concentrate discretionary power in the hands of the few.

▶ ### Denial of Individual Freedoms:
Complete control of speech, press, and assembly limits political dissent and risk of revolution. Criticism of Maoism ended in exile to "re-education" camps. Criticism of "Shariah" ends in death fatwa and persecution.

▶ ### Youth Indoctrination:
Children recruited and converted to Maoism in Schools, and to Sharia-ism in Madrassas. Inner city vulnerable American youth and inmates targeted for radicalization to Sharia-ism.

▶ ### Totalitarian:
Ruled by small groups of self-appointed, power-focused, and unaccountable men; e.g., "Shariah Scholars" and Muslim Brotherhood leaders.

Sharia-ism

 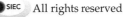

Parallels: *Sharia-ism* and Soviet Communism:
(similar parallels to Fascism)

 insight box Leaders of Soviet Communism, Fascism, and Sharia-ism share a common goal of total control achieved through violence and intimidation, and zero tolerance for political dissent or debate.

▶ **Threat to Physical Safety:**
Those who criticized communism were arrested and tortured as "political prisioners." Criticism of Shariah rule ends in death fatwa.

▶ **Denial of Individual Freedoms:**
Monitoring and control of speech and press and assembly limits political dissent and risk of revolution.

▶ **Imperialist:**
Goal of world domination (referred to as "goal of Caliphate" in Sharia-ism).

Sharia-ism

Male Supremacy is fundamental to both Sharia-ism and South African Apartheid. Women and girls suffer tremendously under both mass movements.

Gender Segregation

Sharia-ism

Male Muslim Supremecy

Racial/Ethnic Supremacy:

White, South African rule created (second class) segregation and oppression of black South Africans. Sharia-ism creates (second class) segregation and oppression of all people, including non-conforming Muslim men, who refuse to comply with the Shariah Manifesto.

Gender Apartheid:

South African Apartheid restricted activities/rights of African Women. Islamic Gender Apartheid entitles husbands and brothers to effectively own their mothers, wives, and sisters. Shariah Islamic Law prescribes legal inequality of Muslim women to Muslim men; e.g., the combined votes of 2-4 women equal one male vote in Shariah Court, paternal custody is enforced for children 9 years and older, wives and sisters must ask fathers or brothers for permission to leave home and/or get an education, oppressive burqua dress codes are enforced.

FREE SOUTH AFRICA

 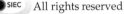

Sharia-ism like Nazism has a goal of world imperialism. In both movements youths are targeted for early indoctrination.

Sharia-ism

 ### Racial/Ethnic Supremacy:
- Aryan, White "Nazi" rule and persecution/death of Blacks, Gypsies, Jews, or anyone who does/did not submit to Nazism.
- Arab Muslim rule and persecution/death of non-Muslims & non-conforming Muslims.

 ### Youth Indoctrination:
- Nazi youth groups.
- Shariah Islamic Madrassa network & targeted prison and inner city youth conversion campaigns in America and Europe.

Imperialist:
- Both share goal of world domination (referred to as "goal of Caliphate" under Sharia-ism).

Sharia-ism seeks control and power by eliminating individual freedoms like these political regimes: Chinese Maoism, Soviet Communism, Fascism, South African apartheid and Nazism. Anyone who refuses to join or comply with any of these political groups are persecuted.

Sharia-ism is very different from these other supremacist movements because it has rooted itself in local, state, and federal areas of influence in America. It's growth is due to:

1. Cover of religious freedom

2. Mid-east oil funding

3. Sharia-enabling American businessmen, lay & government leaders.

4. Silencing of libertarian Muslim opposition through intimidation & threats.

5. Silencing of political debate by using "racist", "islamophobia" and Lawfare campaigns.

Sharia-ism is a political movement containing elements of Fascism, Communism, Chinese Maoism, South African Apartheid and Nazism.

1) *Sharia-ism* seeks to control. Terrorism seeks to destroy. Terrorism is a minor tactic of Sharia-ism.

2) Totalitarian political movements, like *Sharia-ism*. impose rules on members and non-members. Religion imposes rules on members only.

3) The Faith of Islam is protected under Freedom of Religion. The Supremacist political movement of *Sharia-ism* is not protected under the First Amendment.

4) The majority of *Sharia-ists* in American are well educated. They value America and denounce terrorism and destruction. Their goal is to simply shift the American way of life to the *Shariah* way of life, by merging state and mosque.

5) The strategy of *Sharia-ists* in America is to democratically build support for a *Shariah* political party, and elect *Shariah* lawmakers who will merge state and mosque. This is how Nazism and Soviet Communism came to power.

6) The totalitarian movement of *Sharia-ism* has the unprecedented potent combination of: unlimited petrodollar funding and the false cover of Freedom of Religion.

Chapter 4

Sharia-ism: Concepts and Vocabulary:
Apostasy, Blasphemy, Da'Wa, Dhimmitude, Jihad, Taquiyya, Zakat

Reliance of the Traveller: A Classic Manual of Islamic Sacred Law by Nuh
Ha MIM Keller, 1994 edition

Da'wa: An invitation to convert "non-believers" to Islam through friendship, fear, or financial bribery.

Da'wa is found all over the world in Islamic centers, mosques, college campuses and madrassas (public schools). The English translation of Da'wa, "missionary work to bring new believers to Islam, or to reinforce belief," is simplified and misleading, because Da'wa is conducted with intentional deception and intimidation.

Da'wa is not simply Islamic proselytizing. The goal of Da'wa is to force conversion or acceptance of Shariah through means of:

 Deception or lying - Taquiyya

 Intimidation (threats of violence, racial slurs claiming "Islamophobia")

Lawfare (see Chapter 10)

Disingenuous "interfaith dialogue," "building bridges," and "outreach."

 Exploitation of vulnerable groups, such as immigrants, prison inmates, or youth looking for community or power.

Financial payoffs or profiteering opportunities

source: familysecuritymatters.org

CHANGING THE WORLD THROUGH DA'WAH

insight box

Da'Wa is a powerful tactic of Sharia-ism. *Da'Wa* and Jihad and are inextricably linked. They share the same goal of creating global submission to the *Shariah* way of life. *Da'Wa* uses racial slurs, legal threats, and misinformation to lure Americans into accepting *Sharia-ism,* while violent Jihad uses violence or bombs to achieve the same submission.

Da'wa has been termed "cultural Jihad" or "stealth Jihad" by apostates and Muslim Civil Libertarians.

 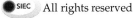

insight box

Most American leaders do not understand that while Da'Wa is a softer, alternative tactic to violent Jihad, it has the same purpose - to achieve Shariah supremacy in America by limiting individual freedoms.

Sheik Qawadawi is a master of Da'Wa. He created a network of 50 Islamic Charities (The Union of Good) which was designated as a terror organization by the U.S. Treasury in 2009. He is also the founder of Shariah Islamic Finance, a banking system which funds global Sharia-ism. In addition, he is currently banned from entering the U.S. because of his ties to terrorism.

In Dec 2011, the Obama administration announced it would "outreach" to the "moderate" Taliban party through its negotiator, Sheikh Qaradawi.

"We will conquer Europe, we will conquer America, not through the sword but through Da'wah (sic) [Islamic proselytizing]."

Yusuf al-Qaradawi,
Muslim Brotherhood Spiritual Leader, Qatar, 1995

"The large number of links between Islamic Relief Worldwide and extremist terror groups suggests that buried beneath the cover of a charity lies a structured pro-terror group with an anti-Western agenda."

www.investigativeproject.org

FREE MEDICAL CLINICS

"ICNA Relief USA established Shifa clinic in 2008 to serve sick in Atlanta area."
www.icnaatlanta.org/shifa-clinic-2

ICNA RELIEF USA
Requests the Joy of Your Presence at the Benefit Dinner and Inspiring Lecture

Relief Efforts Within United States
An Islamic Perspective
Keynote Speaker: Imam Siraj Wahhaj

February 13, 2011

"America is the most wicked government on the face of planet Earth. If only Muslims were clever politically they could take over the U.S. and replace its constitutional government with a caliphate"
–Imam Siraj Wahhaj (photo above), Spokesmen for ICNA Relief USA

Shifa Free Medical Clinics created by Muslim Brotherhood charity group ICNA Islamic Relief USA (IRUSA) are expanding rapidly throughout America. IRUSA based in Wheeler VA. is the American branch of Islamic Relief Worldwide (IRW), located in the U.K.

Some Red Flags:

1 Israel Foreign Affairs designated parent Islamic Relief World as a terrorist front in 2006.

2. Awards to clinic doctors and directors are given by CAIR, identified by the U.S. Treasury as a supporter of Hamas.

3. In November 2012, Swiss Bank UBS shut down the Islamic Relief Charity Bank Account and blocked all new zakat donations due to terror funding concerns.

www.clarionproject.org/analysis/islamic-relief-usa

AWARDS BY HAMAS FUNDER CAIR

CAIR awarded the 2012 Community Service Award to Al Shifa Medical and Dental Clinic in Virginia.

insight box

Health professionals, partnering American charities, and local municipalities who support Muslim Brotherhood Islamic Council of North America (ICNA) Shifa Clinics, packaged under the Islamic Relief USA banner are likely well intentioned. However, good intentions do not eliminate the fiduciary or ethical responsibility of these agents to engage in due diligence and fully disclose the Islamic extremist connections of this Islamic Relief USA charity to patients, donors, patrons , and taxpayers.

Taquiyya:
Strategic Deception

Taquiyya: Deceptive Tactics condoned by **Shariah Islamic Law** (such as misleading, lying, and omitting key facts) used for the purpose and intent of hiding the true goals of Shariah Islam from non-Muslims to fuel Sharia-ism in America.

Taquiyya = Deception or Lying

 Taquiyya may be practiced when Muslims are in the lands of non-Muslims and are not as powerful as those around them.

 It is meant to hide the Muslim's true intentions from non-Muslims.

(Ch. r10.3, p. 748)

 "Scholars say that there is no harm..in giving a misleading impression if required by an interest countenanced by Sacred Law that is more important than not misleading the person being addressed."

(Ch. r10.3, p. 748)

insight box

Most Americans, including American-Muslims, are raised on the faith-based principle of "Thou shalt not lie" along with the popular tales of Pinocchio, and George Washington and the Cherry Tree. The concept of Taquiyya is difficult to believe and, therefore, serves as a very powerful tool of Sharia-ism.

source Reliance of the Traveller, 1994

Taquiyya in Action: Abdurahman Alamoudi
Founder of Islamic Society of Boston Mosque and Center attended by Boston Bomber brothers.

Public statements by Alamoudi

 "We are against all forms of terrorism."

 "Our religion is against terrorism."

Private statements by Alamoudi

 Caught on tape stating that Osama bin Laden hadn't killed enough Americans in the U.S. Embassy bombings.

 Raised funds for al-Qaeda (p. 253, Muslim Mafia)

 Encouraged even more "holy war" and "violent jihad."

"Abdurahman Alamoudi founder of the American Muslim Council in 1990, former Goodwill Ambassador for the U.S. State Dept and Pentagon Muslim Chaplain was described as the "pillar of the local Muslim community" by The Washington Post. In 2004, he was convicted of connections to radical organizations and terror financing through various charities and sentenced to 23 years in jail."

Daniel Pipes, Capitalism Magazine, Aug 2004

Dhimmitude:
Inferior restricted class status

Dhimmitude: the Shariah Islamic system of controlling non-Muslim populations conquered thru Da'Wa or Jihad. Over one hundred Dhimmi laws exist as part of Shariah Islamic law, and describe inferior class status. Certain Dhimmis are permitted to live among the ruling Shariah class if they pay a tax, for the right to be "protected" from death. To avoid Dhimmitude, infidels must convert to Shariah Islam.

Dhimmi Rules: Impose Second Class Status on Non-Muslims in Exchange for Their Right to Life.

Examples of Dhimmi Rules – Non-compliance is punishable by death or persecution.

1 "may not build higher than or as high as the Muslims' buildings."

2 "are forbidden to openly display wine or pork … recite the Torah or Evangel aloud, or make public display of their funerals and feast days;"

3 "are forbidden to build new churches." (Ch. o11.5, p. 608)

insight box

Dhimmitude is described by **Sharia-ists** as "Protection," which sounds kind and benevolent. The Dhimmitude label means that non-Muslims will be "protected" from death and persecution, if they abide by Dhimmitude rules.

These are just a few of the Dhimmi laws. As **Sharia-ists** gain power, more of these rules are imposed.

insight box

In each incident below, Americans accommodate and submit to extraordinary requests of **Sharia-ists** out of fear, intimidation, political correctness or self interest.

* 2006-2009: American Bookstores refuse to carry books critical of Islam out of fear: e.g., Alms for Jihad, Funding Evil, and The Jewel of Medina.

* September 2010: Seattle cartoonist, Molly Norris, is forced to disappear underground after suggesting a "Everybody Draw Mohammed Day" on Facebook. The White House has not condemned her death fatwa, nor supported her right to free speech.

* Ongoing demands met for taxpayer funded charter schools (Brooklyn, NY), foot baths (San Francisco Airport, 2013), and Muslim-only prayer rooms (Denver international Airport, 2013).

* Mayor Bloomberg of NYC, actively supported construction of Ground Zero Mosque and refused to investigate funding and affiliations of Imam Rauf. He disregarded the voices of 70% of Americans who denounced the location of proposed Mosque.

* U.S. Congress, the CIA, and other U.S. Departments continue to work with known Muslim Brotherhood groups like Islamic Society of North America (ISNA), Council on American Islamic Relations (CAIR), Muslim Public Affairs Council (MPAC), and MSA. See Chapter 7, 9, and 13 for more detail.

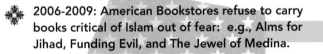

Blasphemy:
Criticism of Islam

Blasphemy: Criticism of Shariah Islamic Law, Mohammad, Allah, by <u>Muslims or non-Muslims (Dhimmis)</u> is a capital offense punishable by death.

Definition of Blasphemy, according to Shariah Islamic Law, which is punishable by death

 1994 updated edition, Reliance of the Traveller

❖ "to revile Allah or His messenger" (Ch. o8.7(4), p. 597)

❖ "to be sarcastic about Allah's name, His command, His interdiction, His promise, or His threat" (Ch. o8.7(6), p. 597)

❖ "to revile the religion of Islam" (Ch. o8.7(16), p. 598)

❖ "to be sarcastic about any ruling of the Sacred Law" (Ch. o8.7(19), p. 598)

❖ "or to deny that Allah intended the Prophet's message ...to be the religion followed by the entire world" (Ch. o8.7(20), p. 598)

Blasphemy laws require Muslim and non-Muslims (Dhimmis) to censor their speech and criticism of Allah. This is a direct violation of the First Amendment which protects Free Speech, including free political speech and debate

Death Fatwas		
Theo Van Gogh Aayan Hirsi Ali	**Netherlands 2004:** Film director of *Submission*, which raised awareness of treatment of women under Islam is murdered. Writer Aayan Hirsi Ali remains in hiding.
Geert Wilders	Wilders, a prominent Dutch politician, was prosecuted on a world platform in 2006 for "hate speech" against Islam. He was acquitted of inciting hatred and discrimination in 2011.
Salman Rushdie	1988 British-Indian novelist wrote *Satanic Verses*. Victim of death Fatwa by Ayotollah Khomeini. Hid for 15 years.
Danish Cartoons	**Denmark 2005:** Kurt Westegard & Lars Vilks created Mohammad cartoons. Still in hiding. Editor of Danish Newspaper burnt to death in March 2010; mysterious fire in his bedroom.

Death Fatwas		
South Park	**New York/California 2010:** South Park TV cable program is labeled 'disrespectful' for mocking Mohammad in cartoon. Parent Comedy Central censored episode after death threats.
2007: Cambridge Press: Publisher of *Alms for Jihad*	*Alms for Jihad* linked Islamic Charity to Jihad. The publisher Cambridge Press recalled books and destroyed inventory.

source: Silenced: How Apostasy and Blasphemy Codes are Choking Freedom Worldwide, Paul Marshall, Nina Shea, 2011

How Apostasy & Blasphemy Codes Are silenced Choking Freedom Worldwide

LOOK INSIDE

Paul Marshall & Nina Shea

Jihad

Jihad: To war against non-Muslims. Derived from the word *mujahada,* signifying warfare to establish the religion.

source: The Legacy of Jihad by Andrew Bostom

Western-non-Islamic countries ▶

2011: Simultaneous atttacks: U.S. Embassies in, Tanzania and Kenya
2001: U.S. Twin Tower, Pentagon
2004: Spain train bombs
2005: Bali Bombing
2005: London Tube bombs
2007: Glasgow airport bomb
2008: Muslim riots: Sweden
2008: Mumbai attack
2011: Morocco bombing
2012: U.S. Embassy: Egypt, Libya
2013: Boston Marathon Bombing

Islamic countries ▶

2006: Iraq mosque bomb.
2009: Pakistan, 40 Coptic houses & church set afire.
2011: Indonesia Mosque bombed.
2011: Pakistan mosque bomb
2011: Eygpt: Coptic Christians killed

insight box

Sharia-ism targets Kafir (non-believers) for death or submission to *Shariah* Islam through *Jihad.* Continue reading Chapter 5 for more examples.

Zakat

Zakat: Money given to charity for the purpose of promoting Islam.

"**Zakat** is not 'charity' as we understand that term... In fact an essential purpose of **Zakat** is to underwrite **jihad**. Americans see it as a dangerous fraud when Islamic charities are used as fronts for terrorist organizations. In mainstream Islam, however, there is no fraud at all — not if your understanding of "charity" is **Zakat**... The stark fact is that the Islamic conception of alms unabashedly embraces what the brilliant scholar of Islam Raymond Ibrahim describes as 'the money **jihad**' (jihad al-mal)."

- Andy McCarthy

Andrew McCarthy - Former Assistant United States Attorney of New York, lead prosecutor in the 1993 Trade Center bombing, Supervisor of U.S. Attorney's Anti-Terrorism Command Post in New York City after Sept 11th, and recipient of Justice Department's highest honors: the Attorney General's Exceptional Service Award (1996) and the Distinguished Service Award (1988).

insight box

Zakat can and does feed the hungry and help the poor. And it also funds Jihad and Da'Wa. Therefore, to translate Zakat, as simply "charity" is misleading. This is an example of Taquiyya, which is a deliberate mistranslation of an Arabic concept to make it more palatable for Westerners. Educating yourself on these facts will help de-rail Sharia-ism in America.

The U.S. Treasury has shut down or designated over 30 Islamic charities as funders of terrorism.

❖ The Reliance of the Traveller defines eight categories of those worthy of receiving Zakat:

1. The poor (h8.8, p. 267)
2. Those short on money (h8.11, p. 269)
3. *Zakat* workers (h8.13, p. 270)
4. Those whose hearts are to be reconciled [political leaders who may embrace Islam] (h8.14, p. 270-71)
5. **Slaves purchasing their freedom** (h8.15, p. 271)
6. Those in debt (h8.16, p. 271)
7. **Those who fight for Allah** (h8.17, p. 272)
8. Travelers [sic] needing money (h8.18, p. 272)

Islamic sources are inconsistent in describing the percentage of Muslim wealth to be tithed. Depending on the source, the required percentage can range from 2.5% - 20%.

source: Reliance of the Traveller

insight box

Note the words of the recently killed al-Qaeda leader and American convert to Islam, Anwar al-Awlaki. He states that Jihadists legitimately qualify for charitable donations or "zakat" according to 4 out of the 8 categories defined on the left side of this page.

"The mujahideen (Jihadists) of today fulfill four out of the eight categories of zakah: They are poor, they are in need, they are wayfarers, and they are the ones in the cause of Allah!"

This is why over 30 Islamic Charities have been designated sponsors of terror in the USA. See next page.

American-born Yemeni cleric and terrorist Anwar al-Awlaki

Designated as Potential Fundraising Front Organizations for Foreign Terror Organizations by U.S. TSY, Exec. Act 13224

insight box — "The terrorist organizations support their activities by fund-raising, often through innocent-sounding charities, non-governmental organizations and by criminal activity." - *Investigative Project on Terrorism*

Afghan Support Committee

Al-Aqsa International

Al Haramain Islamic Foundation

Al-Rehmat Trust

Al-Quds International Foundation

Al-Salah Society

ASAI: Arab Student Aid International

* *Benevolence Foundation Care International, Inc*

Com.de bienfaisance et de sec

Association de Secours Palestinien (ASP)

Elehassan Society

* *The Global Relief Foundation*

* *Goodwill Charitable Organization*

Holy Land Foundation

Imam Khomeini Relief Committee

Iranian Com. for Reconstruction of Lebanon

Islamic African Relief Agency (IARA)

The International Islamic Relief Organization

Islamic Resistance Support Organization (ISRO)

* *Kindhearts*

Martyrs Foundation

Palestinian Association in Austria (PVOE)

Palestinian Relief and Development Fund (Interpal)

Revival of Islamic Heritage Society (RIHS)

Sanabil Assoc. for Relief and Development

* *The Saudi Red Crescent*

Taibah International

Tamil Foundation

* *Wafa Humanitarian Organization*

* *World Assembly of Muslim Youth* (WAMY)

Names of "charities" are deceptively similiar to American Brand name charities.

Apostasy

The desertion, departure or renunciation of Islam is punished with death.
There is no Freedom of Religion or Freedom from Religion under Shariah Law.

Sheikh Qaradawi

 insight box

In 2008, Sheikh Qaradawi issued a death fatwa on Dr. Wafa Sultan, a Syrian-American psychiatrist living in California who condemned Shariah Islam on Al Jazeera and admitted to leaving the Islamic Faith (apostasy). She remains in hiding today. Despite this, the Obama Administration has reportedly reached out to Sheikh Qaradawi to moderate talks between the U.S. and the Taliban according to Al Jazerra TV.

Apostasy from Islam:

❋ **Most serious crime:** "O: Leaving Islam is the ugliest form of unbelief (kufr) and the worst." (Ch. o8.0. p. 595)

❋ **Penalty:** "When a sane person reaches puberty voluntarily apostasizes from Islam, he deserves to be killed. (Ch. o8.1. p. 595)

❋ **Killing an apostate:** "There is no indemnity for killing an apostate (O: ...since it is killing someone who deserves to die." (Ch. o8.4. p. 596)

(Ch. o8.0-8.7, p. 595-98)

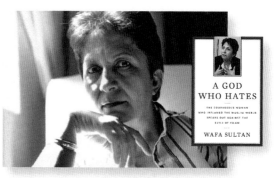

A GOD WHO HATES

THE COURAGEOUS WOMAN WHO INFLAMED THE MUSLIM WORLD SPEAKS OUT AGAINST THE EVILS OF ISLAM

WAFA SULTAN

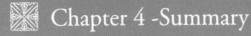

The purpose of this book to expose *Shariah* activities practiced in real time.

This chapter provides definitions of *Shariah* concepts excerpted from the Reliance of the Traveler for academic purposes only.

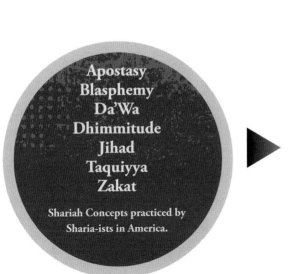

Apostasy
Blasphemy
Da'Wa
Dhimmitude
Jihad
Taquiyya
Zakat

Shariah Concepts practiced by Sharia-ists in America.

1) Muslims who practice the faith of Islam, denounce these *Shariah* concepts and do not participate in the *Sharia-ism* movement. They, like all Americans, believe in individual rights and freedoms.

2) There is often no Western equivalent or English translation of a Shariah concept, which leads to serious mis-interpretations.

3) *Da'Wa* is translated into English as "invitation to Islam." Another English translation is "proselytizing." These translations are inaccurate. *Da'Wa* is the requirement to convert or subjugate non-Muslims through charm, deception, intimidation, persuasion, bribery or *Taquiyya* (outright lying) according to *Shariah* Law.

4) *Taquiyya* is lying or deception. *Taquiyya* is considered by *Sharia-ists* to be a legitimate, sanctioned method of encouraging conversion to *Shariah Islam*, and support of *Sharia-ism*. *Taquiyya* is specifically sanctioned under *Shariah Islamic Law*.

5) *Dhimmitude* is imposed on non-Muslims when *Sharia-ists* or Islamic extremists occupy a region. A *Dhimmi* is a citizen with a lower restricted class status. *Dhimmis* do not have equal rights to Muslim supremacists (*Sharia-ists*). *Dhimmi's* have limited freedom of speech, press, or family life, among many other restrictions. *Dhimmis* are also required to pay a tax or jizyah.

Da'Wa
Taquiyya
Dhimmitude
Blasphemy
Jihad
Zakat

Powerful tactics of Sharia-ism worldwide.

6) *Blasphemy* laws forbid criticism of Allah, Shariah, and Islam by Muslims and non-Muslims alike. Those who violate *blasphemy* laws are victimized with a death fatwa. Blasphemy laws destroy Freedom of Political Speech and Press, protected under the U.S. Constitution.

7) *Jihad*, in English, is translated as "the path." This is an example of an Arabic concept that has no accurate direct translation in English. To understand the concept of Jihad one must look at actions around the world, like the Sept 11th 2001 American mass murder. The *jihad* path is the forced submission or subjugation of all people through holy war.

8) *Zakat*, or the manadatory tithing of earnings is mis-translated to "Charity" in English. Like western "charity," *Zakat* dollars help those in need of food, medical aid, etc. Unlike western "charity," *Zakat* funds the living expenses and operations of non-profit status Muslim Brotherhood groups in America like CAIR, ISNA, and MSA.

9) *Apostasy* laws forbid conversion away from Islam by a Muslim. An Apostate is a Muslim who has converted away from the faith of Islam. There are many American apostates, like Wafa Sultan, who live in hiding or cautiously under death fatwas. The U.S. government is silent on this issue and does not offer any formal protection.

Chapter 5

Sharia-ism: Attacking freedoms of Muslims and non-Muslims globally.

Sharia-ism is a political war lead by radicals from both Sunni and Shiite sects.

"in Brotherhood ideology, the concept of hakimi-yyah signifies Allah's rule through the implementation of the sharia, and what legitimizes the ruler is his implementation of the sharia, not the will of the people expressed when they elect a ruler (Sunni or Shiite)"

The Brotherhood & the Shiite Question, I. Altman, current-trends.org, Nov 2009

insight box

Loyalty to **Sharia-ism** is not the mantle of any sect or group of people. **Sharia-ism** is the mantle worn by extremists. Yes, Sunni and Shia Muslim fight and have differences. This is not **Sharia-ism**.

Sharia-ists share a goal of male Islamic supremacy and world caliphate, and may be Sunni, Shiite, or sanother sect. **Sharia-ists** may or may not formally affiliate with the Muslim Brotherhood.

For example, the Muslim Brotherhood leaders of the **Sharia-ism** movement, historically have been Sunni Muslim. The goverment of Iran, another leader of **Sharia-ism** is Shiite.

Taliban Targets Pakistan mosque

"Christians are the world's most widely perse-cuted religious group, according to studies by the Pew Research Center, Newsweek, and the Economist, among others."
—Persecuted: The Global Assault on Christians. Marshall, Gilbert & Shea

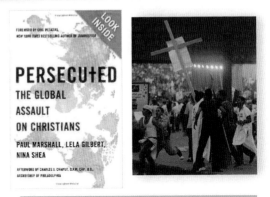

Egypt August 2013: In 3 days, 41 churches and 150 other Christian buildings were attacked by Muslim Brotherhood supporters after the Egyptian military attacked their armed camps. Likely, the largest single pogrom against Egypt's Christians in the last 700 years.

- *Paul Marshall, FOXnews.com*

Nigeria 2013: 10 Catholic church buildings were burned by Islamists . Two Pastors and 46 Christians dead.

- *World Watch Monitor*

Iraq 2013: "Over the past decade, some two-thirds of the Christian population of Iraq has been killed or driven out of the country by targeted extremist violence against 70 of their churches"

- *Nina Shea*
NRO, March 2013

In response to Muslim attacks, there is a mass exodus of Christians fleeing Central Africa, Syria, Iraq, Mali, Bosnia & Pakistan. Reports of :

- 450,000 Christians fleeing Central African Republic. Nov 2012
- Over 200,000 Christians have fled Mali since 2012 Islamic coup.
- 100,000 Christian Copts have fled their Egyptian homeland, since the "Arab Spring.

Raymond Ibrahim, documents this Christian exodus in his book: *Crucified Again; Exposing Islam's New War On Christians.*

insight box

 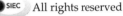

❖ American Airlines Flight 77 crashed into the Pentagon.

❖ **All 58 passengers, four flight attendants, both pilots, and 125 Pentagon workers were killed.**

❖ An estimated 2,600 people worked near the impact site.

❖ United Airlines Flight 93 crashed in Shenksville, PA when passengers fought to take control of the plane from hijackers.

❖ **44 people were killed, including 37 passengers and four terrorists.**

❖ Only hijacked flight that failed to meet its original target: U.S. Capitol, Washington, D.C.

❖ Near simultaneously coordinated suicide attacks, carried out by al-Qaeda terrorists on four passenger planes; second time World Trade Center Twin Towers were bombed.

❖ 2,819 people killed, including 19 hijackers.

❖ Those killed were from 115 nations.

❖ Economic loss to NY in month following attack: $105 billion.

❖ Estimated number of New Yorkers suffering from Post-Traumatic-Stress Disorder as a result of 9/11 attacks: 422,000.

insight box

The Sept. 11 terrorist attacks created more fatalities than any other attack in American history. Nearly 20% of Americans knew someone who was hurt or killed in the attacks.

On April 15, 2013 two hand made pressure cookers bombs filled with nails and scrap metal exploded 13 secs and 210 feet apart at the Boston Marathon Finish Line. Four spectators were killed, 17 people lost limbs and over 264 were injured. Thousands of Spectators and runners continue to experience post traumatic stress. Tsarnaev brothers were charged with massacre.

Is the Massachusetts Attorney General or FBI investigating these facts?

Governor Pat Quinn and Mayor Menino had disregarded warnings of the growing Islamic Society of Boston radicalization hub operating out of the ISB Cultural Center and Mosque. (page 192)

Both Jihad Brothers were connected with the Islamic Society of Boston (ISB) for 18 months prior to their attack. (192)

Imam Faruuq of the Islamic Society of Boston is known for his anti-American rhetoric, and fired as Northeastern University Chaplain in 2013 (page 87)

Massachusetts Attorney General's office accepted $50,000 from radical Imam Faruuq in appreciation of newly created 2010 Islamic Sensitivity Law Enforcement Training program in partnership with Muslim Brotherhood group in 2010. (page 200)

Glen Doherty, a 43 year old ex-Navy SEAL, private security contractor, son, and brother. Glen's dad: "he was a humble hero who never bragged." Glen was a member of the Navy Seal team that rescued Private Jessica Lynch in Iraq in 2003.

Officer Sean Patrick Smith, 34 yrs, a ten-year veteran of the State Department, a husband and a father of two. He enlisted in the U.S. Air Force at age 17 yr.

J. Christopher Stevens was an American diplomat and lawyer who served as U.S. Ambassador to Libya from June - Sept 2012

Tyrone Woods, 41yr, ex-Navy SEAL, husband and father of infant daughter, and two teenage sons. Tyrone's mom: "He had the hands of a healer as well as the arm of a warrior, earning distinction as a registered nurse and certified paramedic."

"America must stay focused on the potential cover up regarding Benghazi. In order for the American people to be assured that the U.S. Constitution Rule of Law was not compromised, the American people must demand a Special Select Committee to investigate the Benghazi Attack."

Lisa Benson October 1, 2013
National Security Speaker
KKNT 960 The Patriot .

❀ **July 2011:** Pvt. Naser Jason Abdo was arrested and charged in July 2011 with planning a terror attack and compiling components for a bomb targeting Fort Hood just weeks after he had been granted conscientious objector status by the Army.

❀ **June 2011:** Two Muslim converts were arrested for planning an attack on a Seattle area military processing center.

❀ **March 2011:** A Muslim immigrant, Arif Uka, opened fire on a bus carrying U.S. soldiers at the Frankfurt, Germany airport, killing two soldiers.

❀ **Nov. 2009:** Major Nidal Hasan killed 13 and wounded 29 in a terror attack at Fort Hood after the Army had been warned about Hasan's contact with al-Qaeda cleric Anwar al-Awlaki.

❀ **2009:** Seven Muslim men from North Carolina were arrested for plotting an attack on the U.S. Marine base at Quantico.

❀ **June 2009:** A Muslim convert and self-described jihadist, Carlos Bledsoe (aka Abdulhakim Mujahid Muhammad), gunned down Army Pvt. William Long and wounded Pvt. Quinton Ezeagwula as the pair stood in front of an Army recruiting center in Little Rock.

❀ **May 2009:** Four Muslim converts from New York were arrested while executing a terror plot that included bringing down military airplanes at Stewart Air National Guard Base.

❀ **May 2007:** Six Muslim men were caught planning and training for an attack on troops at Fort Dix.

❀ **August 2005:** Four Muslim converts were arrested for planning an attack on a California National Guard armory.

Major Nidal Malik Hasan, a U.S. Army trained Psychiatrist, went on a shooting rampage in Fort Hood, TX on Nov. 5, 2009.

 13 dead and 30 injured as a result of attack.

Native of VA; from a Jordanian family; highly educated (MD, MPH)

Hasan was dressed in white robe and skullcap of Muslim imams on the morning of the attack.

Hasan was in touch with his "hero", American cleric in Yemen, Anwar al-Awlaki, #1 U.S. terrorist target at that time.

Hasan was overheard shouting "Allahu Akbar" by witnesses before opening fire. These were the same words shouted by terrorists just before the planes hit the World Trade Center Towers on Sept. 11th, 2001.

The final U.S. Army report did not mention *Shariah* or Islam as the motivation for the attack.

"We recently learned how even the FBI and the military are afraid to investigate connections between Islam's jihad and violence, and it was this fear and politically correct censorship by FBI agents that permitted Major Hasan to carry-on a dialogue about jihad against infidels with the known terrorist Anwar al-Awlaki until Hasan ultimately acted on his Shariah-mandated jihad and murdered 13 Americans and wounded 29 others."

David Yerushalmi - American Freedom Law Center, Senior Counsel

Major Nidal Malik Hasan, 39

Source:A Ticking Time Bomb Counterterrorism Lessons From The U.S. Gov Failure To Prevent The Fort Hood Attack. U.s. Senate Committee On Homeland Security & Governmental Affairs February 3, 2011

Attempted Jihad Attack:

Michigan

Umar Farouk Abdul Mutallab, a 23 year old Nigerian man, attempted to blow up a plane carrying 289 people over Detroit, MI, on Christmas Day using plastic explosives hidden in his underwear. Highly educated engineer—Disciple of U.S.-born Yemeni cleric Anwar al-Awlaki of Dar al-Hijrah.

Umar Farouk Abdul Mutallab

Illinois

American Michael Finton, known as Talib Islam, was arrested for planning to bomb the federal courthouse in Illinois. Finton converted to Islam while serving a sentence in an Illinois prison (2001-2006) for aggravated robbery and battery.

Michael Finton

insight box

Farouk's affluent and highly educated upbringing debunks the myth that Jihadists are poor, uneducated, and lack economic opportunities. Major Hassan, the Fort Hood Army psychiatrist, is another example of an educated, privileged extremist.

Pakistani-American Time Square Bomber with his wife and two children. Neighbors in Connecticut described him as "living a quiet life"..

"If I'm given 1,000 lives, I will sacrifice them all for the life of Allah."

"We are only Muslims ... but if you call us terrorists, we are proud terrorists and we will keep on terrorizing you,"

"We do not accept your democracy or your freedom because we already have Sharia law and freedom."

Statements made by Faisal Shahzad with coverage of trial reported Fox News, May 10, 2010.

May 1, 2010: Shahzad, 31-year-old former budget analyst from Connecticut, lit the fuse of his crude, homemade bomb packed in a 1993 Nissan Pathfinder, then fled on foot. A street vendor spotted smoke coming from the SUV and alerted police. The bomb never went off.

At his trial, New York FBI chief Janice Fedarcyk, said "Shahzad built a mobile weapon of mass destruction and hoped and intended that it would kill large numbers of innocent people and planned to do it again two weeks later."

source: cbsnews.com

insight box

At Shazad's trial, it was uncovered that the Taliban had given him $15,000 and five days of explosive training just months after he became a U.S. Citizen. During his trial, he was asked whether he pledged allegiance to the U.S. at his U.S. Citizen ceremony. Shazad said " I did swear", "but I did not mean it".

Sharia-ism is Political War, not religious war.

1) *Sharia-ism* is a political war for global control lead by radicals who identify as Sunni, Shiite and/or Muslim Brotherhood. Violent *Jihad*, also termed Islamic terrorism is just one tactic of *Sharia-ists*.

2) Muslim women and children (estimated at 1 Billion+) are the largest victimized group by *Sharia-ists*. Few American women rights groups acknowledge or address this.

3) There is a pattern by the U.S. army, judicial, executive and legislative officials, and the media of ignoring *Shariah* driven motivations of attacks, and refusing to use "*Shariah*", Islamic", or "*Jihad*" descriptors. For example, violent Jihadists are simply referred to as "The Foot Hood Shooter," "Boston Bombers" or "Benghazi protesters"in the press and by U.S. Officials.

4) As of July 2011, there have been 52 homegrown jihadist plots or attacks in the United States since the September 11 attacks.

5) Violent *Jihad* against Christians and Hindus in the Middle East and Asia is rampant. Buddhists, Sikh's, and American soldiers are targets as well.

 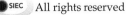

Chapter 6

Two Armed Leadership of Sharia-ism

Arm One: Shariah Clerics in American Mosques & Home-Grown Sharia-ization

Radicalization in the West: The HomeGrown Threat.
Mitchell D. Silber. Arvin Bhatt

The Ulema

Arm One:
The Ulema
Clerics in Mosque Network

❖ Clerics and Mosque Leaders: Imams, Sheikhs, Muftis, Ayatollahs, and Mullahs (both Sunni and Shiite).

❖ Shariah "Scholars" - also referred to as Shariah Advisors, Islamic Scholars, or Shariah Authorities.

Arm Two:
Muslim Brotherhood

❖ International web of groups committed to Sharia-ism.

❖ Highly educated, lay leaders with strategic "day jobs" in the secular world. Hold volunteer leadership positions in political Islamic charities or not-for-profits.

⮡ Salam al-Marayati (MPAC),U.S.

⮡ Ingrid Mattson (ISNA), U.S.

 insight box

This chapter focuses on Clerics who are **Sharia-ists**. These extremists operate out of Mosques, Islamic Centers and Universities with Saudi Funding. It is difficult to estimate how many Clerics reject Sharia-ism because there is little documentation. There is anecdotal evidence, however of increasing pressure on American Imams to support Muslim Brotherhood ideals and Sharia-ism.

Shariah Scholars

❖ *Many Shariah Scholars,* collectively known as the Ulema, are the executive leaders of the anti-freedom movement of *Sharia-ism.* No one has higher authority. Many of these *Shariah champions* carry titles of "Ayatollah, Sheikh, Mullah, Mufti, or Imam."

❖ Only *Shariah* Scholars issue political fatwas which may be directed at Muslims or non-Muslims. *Shariah Law* calls on Muslims to engage in vigilante justice to carry out fatwas. Vigilante justice is illegal under U.S. Law.

❖ *Shariah Scholars* issue financial *fatwas.* Hired as paid board advisory members of banks these *Shariah Scholars* control the use of Muslim and non-Muslim investment funds and the use of Zakat dollars which flow from *Shariah* investments.

American Scholars

American "scholars" are academics involved in research, writing, teaching or consulting.

There is no equivalent American concept to the "Shariah Scholar"; often referred to as an "Islamic Scholar" or "Shariah Authority." There is no equivalent concept or moral equivalence to the concept of issuing legal edicts to kill "infidels" or wage "Jihad."

The "Mapping Shariah" project surveyed 100 randomly selected mosques across the United States.

* 58 percent of the mosques invited guest lecturers known for promoting violent jihad.

* 81 percent of the mosques featured Islamic texts that advocate violence. These texts were available to read or to purchase at these mosques.

* In 84 percent of the mosques, leadership (usually an imam or prayer leader) favorably recommended Islamic texts advocating violence.

Source: Correlations between Sharia Adherence and Violent Dogma in U.S. Mosques. Kedar

*These are the principal takeaways from a study recently competed by Israeli academic Mordechai Kedar and David Yerushalmi of the Center for Security Policy in Washington as detailed in a just-published Middle East Quarterly essay, "Shari'a and Violence in American Mosques."

"The Mapping Shariah study, as its authors observe, may not accurately reflect the whole of Islam in America. Many Muslims do not attend mosques, and those who do are not necessarily receptive to the interpretation of Islam the imams are pushing. The study, however, is a stark depiction of the leadership in Muslim communities."

-Andy McCarthy,
Supervisor of U.S. Attorney's Anti-Terrorism Command Post in New York City post 9-11.

United States Senate
Committee on the Judiciary

"Shia and other non-Wahhabi Muslim community leaders estimate that 80 percent of American mosques - out of a total ranging between an official estimate of 1,200 and an unofficial figure of 4-6,000 - are under Wahhabi control. This does not mean 80 percent of American Muslims support Wahhabism.

Rather, Wahhabi control over mosques means control of property, buildings, appointment of imams, training of imams, content of preaching - including faxing of Friday sermons from Riyadh, Saudi Arabia - and of literature distributed in mosques and mosque bookstores, notices on bulletin boards, and organizational and charitable solicitation. Similar influence includes prison and military chaplaincies, campus activity, endowment of academic chairs and programs in Middle East studies, and most notoriously, to charities ostensibly helping Muslims abroad, many of which have been linked to or designated as sponsors of terrorism. "

Testimony by Stephen Schwartz. Director of Islam and Democracy Program
U.S. Senate Subcommittee on Terrorism, Technology and Homeland Security
Thursday, June 26, 2003

insight
box

If 80% of American Mosques or Islamic Centers are Wahhabi-Saudi controlled, it is reasonable to assume that some enable Sharia-ism? This statement combined with the sample of anti-American quotes by Shariah Imams in this chapter begs these uncomfortable questions:

How many Mosques in America preach Sharia-ism and operate as Shariah Control Centers? How many American Mosques are peaceful houses of prayer?

Should the label "Mosque" or "Islamic Center" automatically qualify for protection under Freedom of Religion, regardless of known radical incitement by Shariah Imams and anti-American rhetoric?

Breaking News: Minnesota teen-jihadis suspected in Kenyan Mall Massacre. September 2013

insight box

The Oct. 2012 trial uncovered an Al-Qaeda affiliated al-Shabab terrorist recruitment pipeline which targets naiive young men to become "American Muslim heroes". Family members are devastated by "brainwashing" of their children.

| Burhan Hassan Age 17 | Shirwa Ahmed Age 27 | Mohamoud Hassan | Jamal Bana Age 19 | Zakaria Maruf | Mustafa Ali Salat Age 18 |

2007-present: At least two dozen Somali-American young men and three young women were reported missing in Minnesota. Since then, an ongoing FBI investigation has confirmed and started to de-construct a pipeline that recruits vulnerable, immigrant American-Somali teens in Minnesota to train and join Jihadist groups in Afghanistan and elsewhere. Minneapolis has the largest immigrant Somali population in America.

Some of these young men have died as suicide bombers in Somalia while some have been arrested in the U.S. Many remain missing. A detailed timeline of the events and investigation as well as biographies of the missing men were constructed and chronicled by Laura Yuen, Sasha Aslanian, and Steve Mullis at Minnesota Public Radio.

❖ Five men, 19 to 25 years of age, from the Alexandria, VA area, were arrested in Sarghoda, Pakistan on terrorism charges.

Police report that they secretly left their homes, families, college classes, and jobs to wage jihad against Americans in Afghanistan, Pakistan and the U.S.

❖ Records showed the five men made contact with a known al-Qaeda operative through social networking sites. Further contacts were likely made through local "on the ground" channels.

Umar Chaudhry, 25

Ramy Zamzam, 22

Waqar Khan, 22

Ahmed Minni, 20

Aman Yemer, 18

insight box

These young American Jihadists came from educated, middle class American families.

Alabama, Georgia, Oklahoma, South Carolina, Tennessee, Virginia

Source: U.S. Justice funded 2006 Report

Excerpts from 2006 U.S. Justice Funded Report:

"Shiekh Gilani has 28 communes spread across the country" " At least a dozen Jamaat ul-Fuqra members have been convicted of terrorist activities"

"Several covert paramilitary training compounds exist within some of the communes. Law enforcement agencies are aware of seven training facilities in the ROCIC region:"

- **Marion Alabama**
- **Commerce Georgia**
- **Macon Georgia**
- **Talihini, Oklahoma**
- **York County, South Carolina**
- **Dover, Tennessee**
- **Red House, Virginia**

"It is common for Jamaat ul-Fuqra to be located near significant infrastructure targets."

(WLRX_TV Reporter notes the Catawba nuclear facility is less than 5 miles from South Carolina commune.)

Sheikh Mubarak Ali Gilani
Muslims of America

"Life is becoming more hard for Muslims, Therefore every man and women should learn to defend himself or herself."

"You can reach us … in upstate New York, or in Canada, or in Michigan, or in South Carolina, or in Pakistan..wherever we are, you can reach us."

Quotes on recruitment videos by international terrorist Sheikh Guliani, founder of terror group Jamaat Al-Fuqra, operating as <u>Muslims of America</u> or <u>Muslims of the Americas</u>.

Sources :
- News 19 video report by WLTX-TV, Islamville, Columbia, South Carolina
- 2006 Law Enforcement Report, written by the Regional Organized Crime Information Center, funded by U.S. Justice Department.
- Christian Action Network
- Lawenforcementtoday.com

Sheriff Bruce Bryant of York Country, S.C.

"We know many people are concerned. But we have a constitution that protects them. They have a right to be there. Many would like to shut them down, but how?"

Muslims of America (MOA) are suing Christian Action Network (CAN) for $30 million for libel. CAN has exposed the MOA recruiting video.

-May 2013

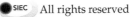

Shariah Imams convert American Mosques to Shariah Control Centers with Saudi dollars, Muslim Brotherhood oversight and anti-American messages.

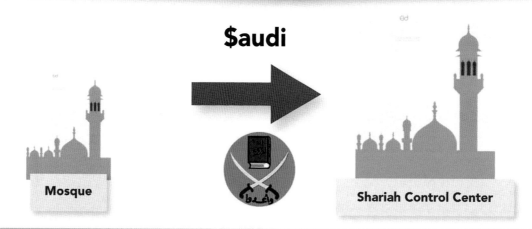

$audi

Mosque

Shariah Control Center

insight box

Ask your close American Muslim friends or colleagues who grew up in the U.S. about their family mosque. You may hear concerns that their mosque leaders are shifting to more fundamental, extreme views. You may hear that they are "mosque-shopping", in search of a more libertarian leadership, or have stopped attending altogether.

There is anecdotal evidence that established faith-based mosques are under pressure to become more Shariah-centric, and many new construction mosques are created with a Shariah mission. It appears that new immigrant Somali, Pakistani or Afghanistani Muslims, are being targeted and indoctrinated into Shariah Command Centers. As of 2003, 80% of American Mosques were Wahhabi controlled and funded. According to ICNA.org, the number of mosques in America has nearly doubled from 1,209 to 2,106 mosques, between the years 2000 - 2011.

Read these next pages to "hear" anti-American messages (publicly sourced) delivered in American mosques by Shariah Imams. Are they preaching religion or politics? Faith or control? Why are these institutions protected under Freedom of Religion? Why are these institutions , known to be operated by Muslim Brotherhood groups given not-for-profit status, which allows them to raise Zakat (charity) dollars to fund their Muslim Brotherhood infrastructure and Shariah Mission?

Northeastern University

Imam Faaruuq of Northeastern University & the Islamic Society of Boston Cultural Center attended by Boston bomber brothers.

"If you help the cause of Allah, he will help you. So there's a word, "Sha'jaa". It means bravery. If anyone is to be brave it must be us. You must grab onto the rope, grab onto the typewriter, grab onto the shovel, grab onto the gun and sword. Don't be afraid to step out into this world and do your job."

AMERICANS for PEACE & TOLERANCE

- Videotape produced by inter-faith group Americans for Peace and Tolerance, cbn.com

Marathon Jihad Brothers

insight box

The Boston bomber brothers attended the Islamic Society of Boston Cultural Center and Mosque operated by the Boston chapter of the Muslim American Society (MAS), "founded as the overt arm of the Muslim Brotherhood in America." as reported by U.S. Federal Prosecutors in 2008. A friend of the younger bomber, Dzhokhan Tsarnaev, says he last saw him at the Islamic Society of Boston there during Ramadan. The mosque says that the older brother, Tamerlan, was an "occasional" attendee over the past year and a half.

The President of Northeastern University terminated Imam Faaruuq, after hearing these violent words and more caught on videotape.

- frontpagemag.com 2013

Shariah Imam Faaruuq

Imam Fawaz Damra, former imam in the Cleveland, Ohio area:

"The first principle is that terrorism, and terrorism alone, is the path to liberation. The second principle is that settlement is decided by the sword."

SOURCE:

D.C. Watson, Letter to Peter King and other members of Congress on behalf of 9-11 Families for a Safe and Strong America, :June 12, 2011,

insight box

Imam Damra was convicted of lying about his ties to Islamic terrorism and is set to be deported.

 **Sheikh Imam Anwar al-Awlaki preached at Dar al-Hijrah Mosque in Falls Church, VA.**

"America as a whole has turned into a nation of evil"

"I eventually came to the conclusion that jihad against America is binding upon myself, just as it is binding on every other able Muslim."

Source: New York Times, 2010.

Sheikh Imam Anwar al Awlaki is an American-born convert to Shariah Islam who preached support of violent jihad against the West, in mosques and through You Tube videos. Imam al-Awlaki was identified as a direct threat to National Security and killed in a targeted U.S. drone attack in 2011. At the Dar al-Hirah Mosque he inspired these home-grown American converts to Shariah-ism :

 Umar Mutallab, Christmas Day underwear bomber

Faisal Shahzad, Time Square car bomber

Nidel Hassan, Fort Hood massacre

Imam Muhammad Al-Asi, former Imam at the Washington, D.C. Islamic Center:

"Now, all our Imams, our public speakers, should be concentrating on militarizing the Muslim public ... Only carrying arms will do this task."

SOURCE:
D.C. Watson, Letter to Peter King and other members of Congress on behalf of 9-11 Families for a Safe and Strong America, :June 12, 2011

insight box **Imam Muhammad Al-Asi advocates the creation of an armed, civilian, Muslim group.**

 **Sheikh Shaker Elsayed, Imam of Dar al-Hijrah Mosque in Falls Church, VA.**

"The enemies of Allah are lining up; the question for us is, 'Are we lining, or are we afraid because, because they may call us terrorists."

"You are a terrorist because you are a Muslim, well give them a run for their money. Make it worth it. Make this title worth it, and be good a Muslim."

Elsayed then told Muslims to accept peace when they receive peace, but to fight back when their families, communities, nations and dignity come under attack.

Imam Elsayed speech before an Ethiopian Muslim group gathered at T.C. Williams High School in Alexandria, Va. Feb 2013.

insight box

Imam Elsayed has been affiliated with Dar al-Hijrah Mosque since 2005. TECS reports dated in 2002, a computer data base operated by U.S. Customs and Border Protection, stated that Dar Al-Hijrah Mosque was "associated with Islamic extremists" and was "operating as a front for Hamas operatives in U.S." TECS reports dated 2007 make similar statements.

Investigative Project on Terrorism, 2010

SOURCE:
Imam Elsayed speech before an Ethiopian Muslim group gathered at
T.C. Williams High School in Alexandria, Va. Feb 2013.

Imam Abdul Alim Musa, Al Masjid Mosque, Washington, D.C.:

"If you don't give us justice, if you don't give us equality, if you don't give us our share of America, if you don't stay out of our way and leave us alone we're going to burn America down."

"Islam went everywhere in the (ancient) world...so why can't Islam take over America?...We are on the right road."

SOURCE:
D.C. Watson, Letter to Peter King and other members of Congress on behalf of 9-11 Families for a Safe and Strong America, :June 12, 2011

insight box Imam Musa is founder of the As-Sabiqun group which advocated for the creation of a global Islamic state that would abolish all "man-made" forms of governance.

Imam Siraj Wahhaj, Masjid Al-Taqwa Mosque, Brooklyn, NY:

"In time, this so-called democracy will crumble, and there will be nothing. And the only thing left will be Islam."

On stoning women: *"If Allah says to stone them to death ... then you stone them to death, because it's the obedience of Allah and his messenger... nothing personal."*

SOURCE:
D.C. Watson, Letter to Peter King and other members of Congress on behalf of 9-11 Families for a Safe and Strong America, :June 12, 2011

insight box

Wahhaj became involved with the Nation of Islam and its leader, Louis Farrakhan, under whose influence he converted to Islam, in 1969. Shortly before the 9/11 attacks, Wahhaj was a guest speaker at a "Jihad Camp" in Pennsylvania. The camp was organized by Safet Abid Catovic, a leader of the Benevolence International Foundation; a "charity" that would be shut down in November 2002 on charges that it had provided funding for al Qaeda.

In 1995, Wahhaj was named by U.S. Attorney Mary Jo White as a possible co-conspirator in the 1993 bombing of the World Trade Center.

Today, Imam Siraj Wahhaj is the spokesman for the Muslim Brotherhood connected charity: ICNA Islamic Relief USA also known as Islamic Relief USA.

Imam Amir-Abdel Malik-Ali: Masjid Al Islam Mosque, Oakland, CA

"From an Islamic movement we graduate to an Islamic revolution," he says. "Then to an Islamic state. . . . We must implement Islam as a totality [in which] Allah controls every place -- the home, the classroom, the science lab, the halls of Congress."

SOURCE:

D.C. Watson, Letter to Peter King and other members of Congress on behalf of 9-11 Families for a Safe and Strong America, :June 12, 2011

insight box

A graduate of San Francisco State University and a former Nation of Islam member, Imam Amir-Abdel Malik-Ali is a frequent guest lecturer at the Muslim Student Union and the Muslim Students Association events. He is a leader in the Al-Masjid and As-Sabiqun movements, which are dedicated to creating an Islamic revolution in the United States.

Imam Fouad El Bayly: Johnstown Islamic Center

Imam Fouad El Bayly

On Dutch author Ayaan Hirsi Ali: "She has been identified as one who has defamed the faith (Islam). If you come into the faith, you must abide by the laws, and when you decide to defame it deliberately, the sentence is death."

SOURCE:
D.C. Watson, Letter to Peter King and other members of Congress on behalf of 9-11 Families for a Safe and Strong America, :June 12, 2011

insight box

Apostate Aayan Hirsi Ali remains in hiding for over 10 years, because death fatwas present real and imminent danger. Shariah Law promotes vigilante justice, which means that **Sharia-ists** everywhere are expected to carry out death fatwas. Aayan is a world leader of women's rights and is featured in the "must see" new documentary Honor Diaries released in March 2014.

Aayan Hirsi Ali

95

Imam Zaid Shakir, former Muslim chaplain at Yale University

"Muslims cannot accept the legitimacy of the existing American order, since it is against the orders and ordainments of Allah."

SOURCE:
D.C. Watson, Letter to Peter King and other members of Congress on behalf of 9-11 Families for a Safe and Strong America, :June 12, 2011

insight box

Imam Shakir appears to speak of taking over America.

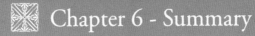

Some Imams in America are cultivating home-grown Soldiers of Sharia-ism.

1) The *Sharia-ism* political movement has two arms of leadership: the Ulema (*Shariah* committed Imams) and the Muslim Brotherhood.

2) A "*Shariah* Scholar" is vastly different than an "American scholar" or "History scholar." As Champions of *Sharia-ism*, *Shariah* Scholars, most with titles of Imam, Sheikh, Mullah or Ayatollah, have the power to issue a death or terror fatwa which is an immediate vigilante call to action. Those who don't enforce this fatwa are subject to be beaten themselves. Even Osama Bin Laden took his orders from a *Shariah* Scholar.

3) This chapter includes a publicly sourced sampling of violent quotes by the Ulema leadership who champion *Sharia-ism* throughout America. These men operate out of Mosques, Islamic Centers and Universities in: Arizona, Massachusetts, California, Connecticut, Georgia, Minnesota, New York, Ohio, Pennsylania, Virginia, and Washington D.C. In their own words these imams call for control of American schools, government, and Congress in order to replace American culture and law with *Shariah* Supremacy and *Shariah* Islamic Law.

4) The Boston Marathon Bombers attended the Muslim brotherhood founded Islamic Society of Boston Cultural Center and Mosque where *Shariah* Imam Faaruuq resides and advocates violence against America.

5) The process and extent of *Sharia-zation* (Radicalization) of vulnerable youth and adults in America is explained with examples.

6) A Study of 100 American Mosques, known as The Mapping *Shariah* project, revealed that 58% - 84% of the sampled American mosques advocate for violence in some manner. Saudi Arabia funds 80% of American mosques which may be a correlation.

 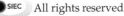

Chapter 7

Two Armed Leadership of Sharia-ism

Arm Two: Muslim Brotherhood Network in America

Report on the Root of Violent Islamist Extremism and Efforts to Counter It: The Muslim Brotherhood, Senate Committee on Homeland Security and Government Affairs, IPT

The Official Muslim Brotherhood MOTTO:

 "The Qur'an is our law;

Allah is our objective;

The Prophet is our leader;

Jihad is our way;

Dying in the way of Allah is our highest hope."

insight box

Muslim Brotherhood members assimilate into society with the purpose of shifting our secular American way of life to a combined "Mosque and State" way of life.

The drawn swords symbolize the brotherhood's willingness to fight for its cause and are a common motif in the flags of Islamic countries.

The Arabic word at the bottom of the circle is waidu, meaning "prepare," and comes from the first word of Qur'anic verse 8:60, which tells Muslims to "Make ready your strength to the utmost of your power, including steeds of war, to strike terror into the hearts of the enemy."

Muslim Brotherhood logo

"To establish an Islamic government on Earth by <u>replacing the U.S. Constitution</u> and British and European common law and establishing parallel Islamic institutions."

Muslim Brotherhood, The Project

1981: Authentic MB written 14 point plan to create a world Shariah Caliphate

Muslim Brotherhood logo

The quote above is taken from the Muslim Brotherhood 1981 written authenticated 14 point plan to create a Caliphate , called The Project. It was discovered by Swiss Intelligence agents months after Sept 11, 2001. This plan virtually mirrors the tactics used by Shariah-ists for more than two decades.

Thanks to journalist Patrick Poole, you can read the English translation of "The Project" (published first) in Front Page Magazine, May 11, 2006.

insight box

U.S. Constitution

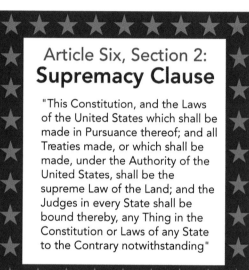

Article Six, Section 2:
Supremacy Clause

"This Constitution, and the Laws of the United States which shall be made in Pursuance thereof; and all Treaties made, or which shall be made, under the Authority of the United States, shall be the supreme Law of the Land; and the Judges in every State shall be bound thereby, any Thing in the Constitution or Laws of any State to the Contrary notwithstanding"

"As it turns out, 'every major Muslim group in the United States is controlled by the Muslim Brotherhood,' veteran FBI agent John Guandolo says... It's not just a loose network of people sharing a common ideology, he says, but a centrally controlled and directed insurgency. 'It's a genuine conspiracy to overthrow the government, and they have organizations to do it, and they have written doctrines outlining their plan,' Guandolo adds."

Gaubatz and Sperry quoting John Guandolo in Muslim Mafia

John Guandolo, Former FBI agent with years of experience investigating the Muslim Brotherhood

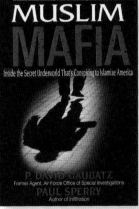

P. David Gaubatz and Paul Sperry, co-authored Muslim Mafia, a revealing look into an undercover investigation of CAIR-The Council of American Islamic Reliations

 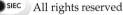

Claire Lopez

"After forcing the FBI and CIA to purge their counter-terrorism training programs of all references to "Islam" in Islamic terrorism, the Muslim Brotherhood in America is focusing on the NYPD" Claire Lopez.

"The Brotherhood's influence within America's own national security leadership circles, academia, and society as a whole already is so great, it can be difficult to realize that the pre-violent jihad by stealth is far more lethal to the West than the violent jihad. The violence will come anyway (at the end), but now is the time for "civilization jihad."

- Claire Lopez, Senior Fellow, Center for Security Policy

For more information, see the online appendix.

"Most Americans do not know about secretly declassified documents detailing their [MB] secret plots to take over the United States from within—a plot launched by Islamist groups tied to the dangerous Muslim Brotherhood, which is based in Egypt and which is funded primarily by wealthy Saudis and Emirates [sic]. And these groups are already in this country, building an impressive infrastructure of support for the Jihadist enemy.

Our elected officials, by and large, are ignorant concerning the threat or afraid to speak out.

The general public is not being told about the danger.

In many instances, our laws are being used against us."

- Sue Myrick, Foreword, Muslim Mafia, (p. i-ii)

Congresswoman Sue Myrick, founded the Congressional Anti-Terrorism Caucus with 120 members.

Representative Myrick was the first member of Congress to speak out against the Shariah-driven Muslim Brotherhood network in America.

After serving in the Congress since 1995, Congresswoman Myrick retired in Jan 2013.

Congresswoman
Sue Myrick (R-NC)

The Muslim Brotherhood known as the "Ikhwan" created its first North American front organization, the Muslim Students Association (MSA), in 1963.

The American Muslim Taskforce on Civil Rights and Elections (AMT) is a Muslim Brotherhood coalition of the 6 groups below:

- (CAIR) Council on American Islamic Relations

- (ICNA) Islamic Circle of North America

- (IIIT) International Institute of Islamic Thought

- (ISNA) Islamic Society of North America

- (MAS) Muslim American Society

- (NAIT) North American Islamic Trust

Muslim Brotherhood Groups in North America. Each has not-for-profit status in the USA, and collects tax-deductible Zakat, or charity, for ongoing operations.

insight box

With the evidence collected at the Holy Land Foundation terror financing trial, the overlapping network of Muslim Brotherhood organizations has become increasingly identifiable.

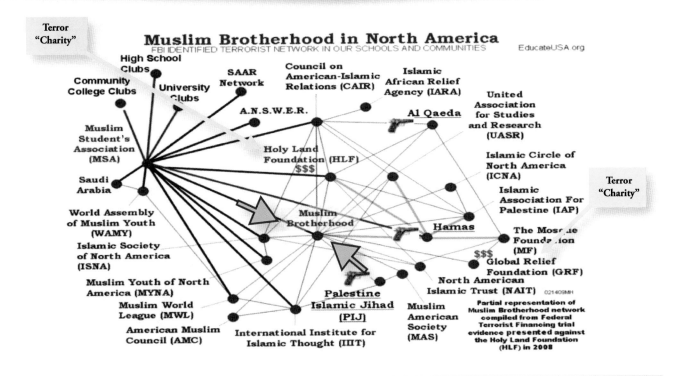

Muslim Brotherhood in North America
FBI IDENTIFIED TERRORIST NETWORK IN OUR SCHOOLS AND COMMUNITIES   EducateUSA.org

Terror "Charity"

Terror "Charity"

High School Clubs
Community College Clubs
University Clubs
SAAR Network
Council on American-Islamic Relations (CAIR)
Islamic African Relief Agency (IARA)
United Association for Studies and Research (UASR)
A.N.S.W.E.R.
Al Qaeda
Muslim Student's Association (MSA)
Holy Land Foundation (HLF) $$$
Islamic Circle of North America (ICNA)
Saudi Arabia
Islamic Association For Palestine (IAP)
World Assembly of Muslim Youth (WAMY)
Muslim Brotherhood
Hamas
The Mosque Foundation (MF)
Islamic Society of North America (ISNA)
$$$ Global Relief Foundation (GRF)
Muslim Youth of North America (MYNA)
North American Islamic Trust (NAIT)
Muslim World League (MWL)
Palestine Islamic Jihad (PIJ)
Muslim American Society (MAS)
American Muslim Council (AMC)
International Institute for Islamic Thought (IIIT)

021409MH

Partial representation of Muslim Brotherhood network compiled from Federal Terrorist Financing trial evidence presented against the Holy Land Foundation (HLF) in 2008

insight box

Note that the Muslim Brotherhood is the hub and at the center of this strategic and powerful network of **Sharia-ist** groups. This partial representation of this MB network was compiled from evidence presented at the Holy Land Foundation (HLF) trial in 2008, where the HLF "Islamic charity" was found guilty of funding Hamas.

Holy Land Foundation Trial

Ghassan Elashi - Founding Director of CAIR:

Sentenced to 65 years for funnelling funds to HAMAS.

Mohammad El-Mezain - Holy Land Foundation leader, CA:

Sentenced to 15 years for funnelling funds to HAMAS

Shukri Abu Bakr - President of Holy Land Foundation:

Sentenced to 23 years for funnelling funds to HAMAS

insight box

The HLF, or Holy Land Foundation, trial was the largest trial involving the prosecution of terror financing in U.S. history. "Prosecutors determined that HLF illegally channelled more than $12 million to the Palestinian terrorist group [HAMAS] through donations to a series of charities, or *zakat* committees", according to the Investigative Project on Terrorism.

CAIR, ISNA, and NAIT were designated as unidicted co-conspirators along with nearly 300 other entities/individuals as co-conspirators and are identified as fronts for the Muslim Brotherhood as part of a domestic network bankrolling Hamas, a US-designated terror organization.

The Investigative Project on Terrorism founded by Steve Emerson provided essential documentation for the successful conviction of the HLF.

investigativeproject.org

"*The Muslim Student Association at most schools is a front for Hamas and the Muslim Brotherhood. Because it is a front organization in the classic communist sense, it poses as a cultural religious group (non-political) in order to promote a false image, which has political advantages and to recruit activists to its more sinister causes. Many innocent students and university administrations get fooled.*"

- David Horowitz
Civil rights activist, and author.
Founder of the David Horowitz Freedom Center
(editor-in-chief of Front Page Magazine).

"*There is overwhelming evidence that the MSA, far from being a benign student society, is an overtly political organization seeking to create a single Muslim voice on U.S. campuses—a voice espousing Wahhabism, anti-Americanism, and anti-Semitism, agitating aggressively against U.S. Middle East policy, and expressing solidarity with militant Islamist ideologies, sometimes with criminal results.*"

- White Paper by Jonanthan Dowd-Galley
Published in Middle East Quarterly, Spring 2004

insight box

The MSA, as the first Muslim Brotherhood front group created in America, has over 600 U.S. College and University members. University Trustees and Administrations across the USA, are un-educated or willfully blind to this extremist network on their campuses, and are enablers of incubating Sharia-ism on college campuses.

 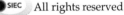

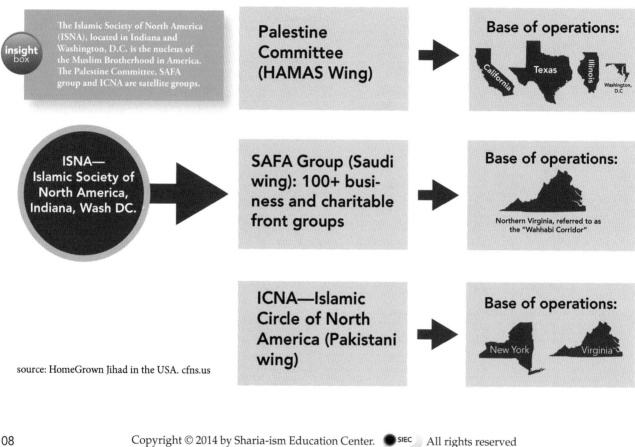

insight box

The Islamic Society of North America (ISNA), located in Indiana and Washington, D.C. is the nucleus of the Muslim Brotherhood in America. The Palestine Committee, SAFA group and ICNA are satellite groups.

Palestine Committee (HAMAS Wing)

Base of operations:

California Texas Illinois Washington, D.C

ISNA— Islamic Society of North America, Indiana, Wash DC.

SAFA Group (Saudi wing): 100+ business and charitable front groups

Base of operations:

Northern Virginia, referred to as the "Wahhabi Corridor"

ICNA—Islamic Circle of North America (Pakistani wing)

Base of operations:

New York Virginia

source: HomeGrown Jihad in the USA. cfns.us

U.S. Dept of Defense and U.S. Dept of Prisons has given exclusive certification and training of Muslim Chaplains to ISNA and GSISS groups, both identified as key Muslim Brotherhood front groups by the Dept of Justice during the 2008 Holy Land Terror Financing case.
The Islamic Society of North America (ISNA) is based in Indiana, and the Graduate School of Islamic and Social Sciences (GSISS) is based in Virginia.

FACT: Saudi money finances an extensive outreach program to U.S. prisons, sending money and tens of thousands of Qu'rans to organizations such as the National Islamic Prison Foundation, for the specific purpose of converting prisoners to jihad.

freerepublic.com, Sept 2006

"Prisons continue to be fertile ground for extremists who exploit both a prisoner's conversion to Islam while still in prison, as well as their socioeconomic status and placement in the community upon their release."

Robert Mueller
FBI Director, 2005 address to a Senate Intelligence committee

Vendredi 6 décembre 2013

One of Egypt's most widely-read newspapers El-Watan published a list of 30 alleged Muslim Brotherhood activists and entities operating "as a Lobby" in America. The article was written by journalist Ahmed al-Tahiri, with direct translation by Raymond Ibraham.

According to sources of Ahmed al-Tahiri, one task for this lobby was to win White House support for the Muslim Brotherhood Morsi government. They succeeded.

Reproduced exactly from frontpagemag.com and clarionproject.org:

- Union of Egyptian Imams in North America, represented by Sheikh Muhammad al-Bani
- The Egyptian American Foundation for Development
- Dr. Khalid Lamada, New York
- Dr. Hassan al-Sayah, Virginia
- The Egyptian Network in America, led by Dr. Muhammad Helmi
- Dr. Akram al-Zand, Sa'ad Foundation
- Muhammad al-Khashab, Head of ART channels in America
- Sameh al-Henawi, member, Business Association of America
- Dr. Hany Saqr, member, Egyptian Association in America
- Dr. Khalid Hassan, Maryland
- Dr. Muhammad Abdel Hakem, Seattle
- Dr. Ahmed Ismat al-Bendari, President, Islamic Society of America
- Walid Yusari, Chicago
- Ahmed Shadid, New Jersey
- Ahmed al-Hatab, Indiana
- Dr. Muhammad Morjan, Boston
- Ramadan Ridwan, Houston
- Ahmed Fayez, Las Vegas
- Dr. Amru Abbas, member, Egyptian Foundation in Michigan
- Dr. Safi al-Din Hamed, Pennsylvania

- Dr. Hamdy Radwan, North Carolina
- Ahmed Shehata, Director, Egyptian American Organization for Democracy and Human Rights
- Dr. Iman Shehata, New York
- Dr. Muhammad Amru Attawiya, member, Organization of Islamic Relief in the United States
- Dr. Khalid al-Sayes, member, Rebuilding of Egypt Foundation
- Dr. Iman Shehata, New York
- Dr. Muhammad Amru Attawiya, member, Organization of Islamic Relief in the United States
- Dr. Tariq Hussein, member, American Islamic Relations Council (CAIR)
- Dr Hisham al-Gayar, member, Egyptian Foundation, Michigan
- Amin Mahmoud, Maryland

Congressman Frank Wolf

Sept. 2013. Congressman Frank Wolf (R-VA) wrote a scathing letter to FBI director James Comey regarding the Department of Justice report that numerous FBI offices continue to maintain relationships with CAIR. No congressional action has been take as of December 31, 2013.

"blatant disregard of bureau policy"... "with respect to (on-going) interactions by the FBI with CAIR."

'I am asking you to immediately remove any FBI agents or any employees that knowingly violated this policy or ..who approved and carried out actions that directly contravened established policy and law – and report to the Congress on what disciplinary actions are being taken."

Congressman Frank Wolf, Press Release, wolf.house.gov, Sept 19, 2013

Good News:

On Nov 14, 2011, President Obama signed H.R. 2112 into law. It included a provision that prevents the FBI from working with the unindicted co-conspirators who enabled the funding of Hamas in in the Holy Land Foundation Trials, including these 3 powerful Muslim Brotherhood American-based groups: CAIR, ISNA and NAIT.

Bad News:

FBI violates law and continues to appease MB groups.

For example:

In Feb 2012, the FBI under pressure from CAIR and ISNA, purged 700 documents and 300 presentations of offensive language such as "jihad" or "Shariah" or "Islam", to appease Muslim Brotherhood Groups in America.

The decision on what language to purge was based on four criteria: 1) "factual errors" (i.e. defining Jihad as holy war is considered a factual error), 2)"poor taste", 3) use of Arab stereotypes (i.e. describing the goal of Muslim Brotherhood as world domination is considered stereotyping) , 4) or "lack of precision".

General Attorney Eric Holder and FBI Director Robert Meuller approved this purge of politically incorrect language found in existing counter-terrorism and intelligence documents.

The Muslim Brotherhood is the second arm of Shariah leadership globally and in America.

1) The Islamic Society of North America (ISNA) is the nucleus Muslim Brotherhood group in America, with three powerful branches supported by Hamas, Saudi Arabia and Pakistan. The name of the Pakistani branch is the Islamic Circle of North America (ICNA).

2) The FBI, Congress, White House, the U.S. Military, and U.S. Prison leaders continue to engage with Muslim Brotherhood Organizations which claim "moderacy," yet have a *Shariah*-driven agenda; such as Islamic Society of North America (ISNA), Council of American Islamic Relations (CAIR), and Muslim Public Affairs Council (MPAC).

3) Despite everything presented in this chapter, and dozens of additional sources authenticating the infiltration of the Muslim Brotherhood in America, the Department of Justice (DOJ) refuses to prosecute Muslim Brotherhood groups under RICO statutes.

4) Mainstream American media has played a significant role mis-informing and mis-representing the Muslim Brotherhood to Americans and conflating the religion of Islam with the political movement *Sharia-ism*.

Chapter 8

Sharia-ism suffered by Women and Children in America.

Honor Murders: Middle Eastern and South Asian cultural practice whereby a family member, usually female is murdered by other family members, in pre-meditated way for "shaming" the family. Examples of "Shame" are: asking for divorce, wearing western clothing, disobeying father or husband.

Forced Marriage, Nikah. According to Shariah Islamic Law: arranged marriage contract is negotiated for brides as young as 9 years old and silence is consent. Bride resisting an arranged marriage risks death.

Polygamy: A Muslim man has the right to have up to four wives. A Muslim woman may have only one husband.

Wife Beating: Husband may beat his disobedient wife but not about the face.

Divorce: is a man's privilege. He may divorce by telling his wife three times, "I divorce thee." with no due process of law.

Child Custody: Mother has custody until child is 9 years old, when Father is given permanent custody.

One of the "Harry Potter" actresses, Afshan Azad, (who plays the graceful and lovely Padma Patil), was recently threatened with death by her father and brother because she was dating a Hindu man. They beat her up, causing her to flee her home and go into hiding in London. Afshan's family is Muslim and from Bangladesh.

insight box

While honor killings are not committed only by Muslims, a 2010 study in Middle East Quarterly, reports that 84% of those who have committed honor murders in North America have been Muslims and 96% of honor murderers in Europe were Muslims. Wives and daughters are honor-murdered for not following Shariah Law which demands their submission to husbands and sons. Over the past four years, American-Muslim women have been honor-murdered in America for asking for divorce, wearing western clothes, socializing with non-Muslim men, and refusing to wear a veil.

 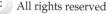

"The most dangerous aspect of this case is to simply say it is domestic violence."
- Dr. Zuhdi Jasser, AIFdemocracy.org

Feb. 2009: Mrs. Assiya Hassan was stabbed 40 times in face, back and chest and then decapitated by her TV Executive husband Muzzammil Hassan. In 2004, Mr. Hassan founded Bridge TV to combat the negative stereotype of Muslims post-9/11, and show the modern face of Islam. His wife was general manager.

When Hassan killed his wife, their then 4- and 6-year-old children were buckled into car seats outside in a van. His wife had been on her way to take them to dinner when she ran into the TV station to drop off his laundry.

Mr. Hassan was charged with second degree murder and sentenced 25 years to life in 2011.

BEHEADED

Assiya Z. Hassan | Muzzamil Hassan

insight box

"The fierce and gruesome nature of this murder signals that this is an honor killing. The display of body parts is a public message that he was in control of his wife."

Source: Dr. Phyliis Chesler is an expert on Islamic Gender Apartheid and Professor of Psychology. In 2013, she published her memoir: An American Bride in Kabul, which is her story of being a 19 year-old American bride living in Afganistan with her Muslim husband and his family.

Honor Killing Arizona 2009: Not Considered First Degree Pre-Meditated Murder in U.S. Court. Difference Between Domestic Violence & Honor-Killing Misunderstood.

Twenty year old Noor Almaleki, who lived in Arizona for sixteen years, wore make-up and western style clothing. Her father had recently become an American citizen. Ashamed of his daughter's dress and style, he took Shariah Islamic Law into his own hands and "honor-murdered" his own daughter. While Noor was on a date, her father gunned the family jeep to thirty miles per hour and ran over both his daughter and her friend. He backed up and ran over Noor a second time as she lay bleeding, this time fracturing her face and spine. Noor died days later. Noor had plans to leave home soon, because her father had threatened to kill her several times. Noor's friend, Amal Khalaf, was thrown 27 feet, fracturing her pelvis and femur. She survived.

Public Defender Billy Little argued **against** seeking the death penalty on the grounds of supposed bias by the prosecution and instead requested **"An open process [that] provides some level of assurance that there is no appearance that a Christian is seeking to execute a Muslim for racial, political, religious or cultural beliefs,"** referring to County Attorney Andrew Thomas' Christian faith.

insight box

In Feb 2011, Noor's father, Faleh Almaleki, was convicted of second degree murder. Despite having threatened his daughter with death multiple times, and running over her twice, the jury did not believe that this father planned to kill his daughter that day. This jury and judge may have viewed this murder as extreme domestic violence, which is vastly different from honor killings. World expert, Dr. Phyliss Chesler, expert in Islamic Gender Apartheid explained that "in the West, wife batterers are ostracized and domestic violence is seldom celebrated."

To the contrary, in the West and East, Muslims who commit or assist in the commission of honor killings view these killings as heroic and even view the murder as the fulfillment of a religious obligation. Honor killings are not stigmatized. While Islam does not condone honor killings, many sheikhs still preach that disobedient women should be punished. Few sheikhs condemn honor killings as anti-Islamic."

Read more: "Are Honor Killings simply Domestic Violence?" Middle East Quarterly, 2009.
Phylis Chesler is a world expert on Islamic Gender Apartheid & Honor Killing and co-founder of the Association for Women in Psychology and the National Women's Health Network.

Honor Killings in Texas, New York, Illinois Georgia, Ohio, Canada, and the U.K.; Victims Punished for being too "Western"

Amina & Sarah Said, 17 yrs.

2008 Texas: Teen sisters, shot to death by their Egyptian father on New Year's Day for "adopting a Western lifestyle and dating American boys"

Sandeela Kanwal, 25 yrs.

Georgia (2008): Father strangled daughter with bungee cord for wanting to leave arrange marriage.

Aasiya Z. Hassan, 37 yrs.

2009 New York: Beheaded by Pakistani husband for wanting a divorce. Second degree murder charge

Tawana Thompson, 19 yrs.

Illinois (2010): Shot to death along with 3 children by husband, who had converted to Islam in prison, for wearing western clothing.

Morsal Obeidi, 16yrs.

Germany (2008): Sister stabbed 20 times by brother for her western ways.

Khatera Sadiqi 20 yr. fiance, Feroz Mangal

Canada (2006): Shot to death by Sadiqi's brother for getting engaged without father's consent.

Sabina Akhtar, 26

U.K. (2008): Stabbed to death by husband.

Methal Dayem, 16 yr.

Cleveland (1999): Shot to death by male cousins

 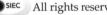

Honor Killings in Texas, New York, Illinois Georgia, Ohio, Canada, and the U.K.; Victims Punished for being too "Western"

Shafi sisters Zainab 19, Sahar 17, and Geeti, 13 - First wife, Rona Amir 50 yr

Aqsa Parvez, 16 yrs

Riza family: Carneze 39, Sayrah 16, Sophia, 15, Alicia, 10, and Hannah, 3

Uzma Rahan, 32, sons Adam, 11, Abbas 8 and daughter Henna six

Canada (2009): Three daughters and their father's first wife were trapped & drowned in a canal by their father, his second wife, and their brother.

Canada (2007): Strangled in family home by father and brother.

U.K. (2006): Wife and four daughters were burned to death by their father, who threw and lit petrol on them while they slept.

U.K. (2007): Mother & three children were beaten to death with a bat by the father who claimed his wife had an affair.

insight box

Study by Dr. Phylis Chessler concluded that 91% of honor killings worldwide are conducted by Muslim families who are importing this practice into America & Europe. While some Sikh and Hindu practice honor-murder in India, America Sikhs and Hindus have not imported this practice into their adopted western homes.

3000

Known or suspected cases of Forced Marriages across 47 United States in 2009-2011.

The Tahirih Justice Center is a national non-profit legal advocacy org which protects immigrant women and girls in America fleeing violence and forced marriage.

Source: Tahirih Justice Survey on Forced Marriages in Immigrant Communities in the US. Sept. 2011

insight box

The AHA Foundation founded by Honor crime expert Phylis Chessler, apostate Aayan Hirsi Ali report that American girls are being flown overseas to forcibly marry a "relative" of some kind. American Girl returns home as enslaved bride and new Sharia-ist husband becomes American citizen.

On February 22, 2011, Jessie Bender, a 13 year-old white, California girl, ran away from home. Jessie was terrified that her American-born mother, Melissa, a convert to Islam, and her mother's Pakistani boyfriend and acting stepfather Mohammed "Mo" Khan, had decided to send her to Pakistan to be married against her will.

Estranged family member said , she "was going to be married off to [the stepfather's] brother over in Pakistan because he was in some trouble and they wanted to bring him over to the states. They were going to get paid $3000 for this".

Frontpagemag.com 2011

"They have to cook for them, wash their clothes, everything. They are still attending schools in Islington (U.K.) struggling to do their primary school homework, and at the same time being practically raped by a middle-aged man regularly and being abused by their families. **So they are a wife, but in a primary school uniform."**

"The reason it doesn't get out is because they are too terrified to speak out, and also the control their families have over them is impossible to imagine if you're not going through it. The way it is covered up is so precise, almost unspeakable."

Dianna Nammi, Director of Iranian and Kurdish Women's Rights Organization (IKWRO), speaks of forced marriage in U.K.

IKWRO, reported there had been almost 3,000 "honour-based" Shariah violence cases in Great Britain in 2010 including forced marriages of children 9 - 16 yrs.

This is a photograph of Muslim girls studying in a British school as an example of the child brides described to the left. The background of these particular girls is unknown.

Photograph: David Sillitoe for the Guardian

insight box

There are common forced marriage scenarios in western countries: 1) Child is sent abroad and returns home with an Islamic Marriage and husband receives gift of a visa or citizenship, 2) Child sent abroad and forced to remain with husband in Islamic marriage in his native country, 3) Child forced into Islamic marriage conducted in western Shariah court, and continues to live in adopted home country. In 2009, The UK government estimated 5000-8000 forced marriage cases.

Faces of Silence

An IowaWatch special report

This project was the master's thesis for Lamia Zia at the University of Iowa School of Journalism and Mass Communication in fall 2012. Zia interviewed domestic abuse survivors living in a Chicago shelter, experts, local women and Imams. She worked with the Peaceful Families Project, a national group devoted to ending abuse in Muslim families.

IowaWatch.org

> Studies of abuse among Muslim women in America range from 30-41%. There are 300,000 Muslim women living in Chicago area, by extrapolation 100,000+ are abused.
> *IowaWatchOrg 2013.*

Interview Excerpts of American Muslim women living in mid-west:

"Despite the fact we know our rights in the U.S., we cannot go against our men"

"What stops us from taking any steps or remaining silent is our cultural values and social pressures.

We have been taught to compromise and sacrifice for the sake of children. In fact, we don't realize that our children become mentally sick and badly affected."

"I always remained silent and never complained but that day, I decided to run away, but did not know where to go." "I came to this shelter, and took a sigh of relief,"

How to help:

Reach out to your immigrant women neighbors. Help them understand and experience the freedoms and rights of women in America for themselves and their daughters. The hope is that second generation American Muslim women will not tolerate forced submission to their husbands or sons under Sharia-ism.

- Joy Brighton

HONOR DIARIES
CULTURE IS NO EXCUSE FOR ABUSE

Nine brave activist women (7 Muslim, 1 Sikh, 1 Christian), now living in the west, describe their brutal personal stories of gender inequality, forced marriage and human rights abuse in their native countries. The growing problem of Honor Violence in America is discussed. A powerful must see.

Since chilling comments by CAIR (see right) , the Canadian, American & Muslim women in the Honor Diaries movie been seriously threatened on social media. And Univ. of Michigan, Illinois and Chicago have shamefully cancelled screenings. CAIR's actions hurt Muslim Women.
Will National Organization of Women (NOW), the largest American women's rights group , step up for Muslim women living under Sharia-ism in America, and screen educational Honor Diaries film to 500 local & college campus chapters?
Will NOW lobbyists pressure Attorney General Eric Holder & Congress to sever ties with American anti-feminist group CAIR?

CAIR
Council on American-Islamic Relations

"The problem with this film is that these producers have a track record of promoting anti-Muslim bigotry, are highjacking a legitimate issue to push their 'hate-filled agenda".

Message from CAIR to Fox News, March 31.

"Civil Rights Advocacy is at the Center of CAIR's work" cair.com April 2014

Cancelled film screenings

"If it is anti-Muslim to raise awareness about the human rights violations occurring against Muslim women in the UK, Canada, & USA, and in Pakistan and the Muslim world ...what then is pro-Muslim?
Response to CAIR by Brooke Goldstein filmmaker , Human Rights attorney & founder of The Children's Rights Institute.

"The issue of Honor Violence is a manufactured controversy in America only, by political extremist front groups, that's how I would describe CAIR. We have women recently being honored in Saudi Arabia and Pakistan for their work exposing honor violence".

Qanta Ahmed,MD. Featured in Honor Diaries Author: Land of Invisible Women: A Female Doctor's Journey into the Saudi Kingdom..

"Honor is a harmless word that replaces...male control over female"

—Manda Zand Ervin
U.S. Delegate to U.S. Commission on Status of Women

"It is very difficult to describe Honor through the lens of a someone raised in Western culture".

Aayan Hirsi Ali
Named in 2005 by Time magazine as one of the 100 most influential people in the world

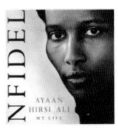

In the past four years and in the name of "Honor," women and girls have been forced into marriages, honor-murdered, genitally mutilated, physically abused, or be-headed in Iowa, Arizona, Texas, New York, Illinois, Georgia, Ohio, and at least 39 other states in America.

Nazanin Afshin-Jam

Aayan Hirsi Ali is a black, Somalian, Muslim raised woman, genitally mutilated at age 5 and more. She fled forced marriage in 2002 and has devoted her life to defending the rights of women and girls in the west from oppression justified by religion and culture - the mission of her 2007 AHA foundation. And, since 2002, she lives in the shadows, in fear of her death fatwa (mandated by Shariah Law) for criticizing Islam and converting away.

On April 8, the president of Brandeis University, Fredrick Lawrence rescinded Aayan Hirsi Ali's invitation to be the Key Note speaker and receive an honorary degree at the May 18 Class of 2014 graduation. Eighty-five of 350 faculty and 6000 students actively pushed for Aayan's dismissal. Why? Because she is a harsh critic of Islam.

Louis Brandeis, namesake of this University, who said that "sunlight is the best disinfectant" is forever disgraced.

Will benefactors ,women college students & Pulitzer prize winning journalists sit by as their alma mater shuts down the voices of abused Muslim women, violates Free Speech and degrades an International Champion of Women's Rights?

"Change can only happen through dialogue, if we don't talk about the abuses taking place, nothing will change."

Iranian born activist Nazanin Afshin-Jam is founder of Stop Child Executions Campaign

Honor Diaries is narrated by nine courageous women's rights activists who tell their own stories and expose the institutionalized abuse of women and girls sanctioned by culture, religion, sharia or any other unacceptable excuse.

| Nazanin Afshin-Jam | | Fahima Hashim | | Raheel Raza | | Raquel | | Manda Zand Ervin |
| Nazie Eftekhari | | | Zainab Khan | | Jasvinder Sanghera | | Juliana Taimoorazy Council | |

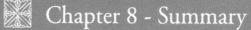

THERE **CAN BE**
NO **CAN BE**
HUMAN RIGHTS
WITHOUT
WOMEN'S RIGHTS

American Women and Children abused under Sharia-ism

1) *Shariah*-based practices being forced upon American women:
   - As many as 3000 forced marriages uncovered in America in 2011 survey.
   - American teens & women being honor-murdered for asking for divorce, wearing western clothes, and more.
   - 25% of Muslim women living in America may be beaten according to Turning Point, a non-profit agency to address domestic abuse among Muslim women.
   - 2009 Sound Vision stats: " Based on the few studies that we have about Muslims in America, we know 30-40% experience emotional abuse.

2) Study By Phylis Chessler concluded that 91% of honor killings in world are conducted by Muslim families who are importing this practice into America & Europe. While some Sikh and Hindu practice honor-murder in India, America Sikhs and Hindus have not imported this practice here.

3) 2014 Honor Diaries Documentary exposes the brutal human rights abuses described in this chapter.

   CAIR shows its true colors as a leading Sharia-ist group in America, and calls filmmakers "anti-Muslim BIgots". Muslim Brotherhood connected MSA College Chapters join Islamophobia campaign.

   The University of MIchigan, Chicago & Illinois cancelled screenings. In April 2014, Brandeis University revokes honorary degree upon Aayan Hirsi Ali, featured in film as champion of women's rights, despite living under death fatwa for 12 years for "defaming Islam". Where is the outrage by women on every college campus? Where are the national women's rights groups like NOW?

Chapter 9

**Creeping *Sharia-ism:*
Strategy to Sharia-ize and control America in small steps.**

Creeping + *Sharia-ism*

=

"**The slow, deliberate, and methodical advance of *Sharia-ism* in non-Muslim countries**" with the long term goal of gaining political, social and economic control over sovereign nations and replacing country law with Shariah law. This is best done by democratically electing a Sharia-ist party, and slow merge of mosque and state.

Synonyms: *"Stealth Jihad," "Soft Jihad," and "Cultural Jihad"*

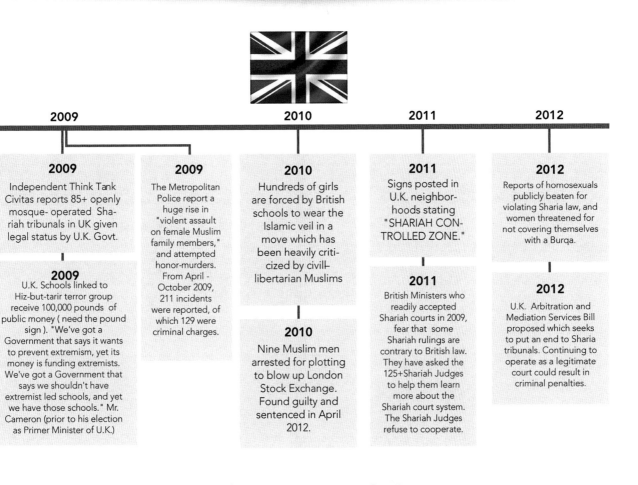

2009   **2010**   **2011**   **2012**

2009
Independent Think Tank Civitas reports 85+ openly mosque- operated Shariah tribunals in UK given legal status by U.K. Govt.

2009
U.K. Schools linked to Hiz-but-tarir terror group receive 100,000 pounds of public money (need the pound sign). "We've got a Government that says it wants to prevent extremism, yet its money is funding extremists. We've got a Government that says we shouldn't have extremist led schools, and yet we have those schools." Mr. Cameron (prior to his election as Primer Minister of U.K.)

2009
The Metropolitan Police report a huge rise in "violent assault on female Muslim family members," and attempted honor-murders. From April - October 2009, 211 incidents were reported, of which 129 were criminal charges.

2010
Hundreds of girls are forced by British schools to wear the Islamic veil in a move which has been heavily criticized by civill-libertarian Muslims

2010
Nine Muslim men arrested for plotting to blow up London Stock Exchange. Found guilty and sentenced in April 2012.

2011
Signs posted in U.K. neighbor-hoods stating "SHARIAH CONTROLLED ZONE."

2011
British Ministers who readily accepted Shariah courts in 2009, fear that some Shariah rulings are contrary to British law. They have asked the 125+Shariah Judges to help them learn more about the Shariah court system. The Shariah Judges refuse to cooperate.

2012
Reports of homosexuals publicly beaten for violating Sharia law, and women threatened for not covering themselves with a Burqa.

2012
U.K. Arbitration and Mediation Services Bill proposed which seeks to put an end to Sharia tribunals. Continuing to operate as a legitimate court could result in criminal penalties.

The bright yellow messages posted on bus stops and street lamps have been seen across certain boroughs in London. Posters deem the targeted area to be a "Shariah Controlled Zone" demand:

'no gambling', 'no music or concerts', 'no porn or prostitution', 'no drugs or smoking' and 'no alcohol'.

- Dailymail.co.uk, July 2011

This campaign was created and carried out by ISLAM4UK, led by British-born convert to Islam, Anjern Choudary.

In November 2011, Home Secretary Theresa May Member of Parliament ordered a ban on the group, Muslims Against the Crusades making membership a criminal offense based on their Islamic Emirates Project.

Muslims Against the Crusades has launched an Islamic Emirates Project naming these 12 British cities to operate as autonomous enclaves ruled by Shariah Law, outside of f British Jurisprudence: Birmingham, Bradford, Derby, Dewsbury, Leeds, Leicester, Liverpool, Luton, Manchester, Sheffield, Waltham Forest and Tower Hamlets are targeted for blanket Sharia rule.

source:
theguardian.com 2011

insight box

France is the first country in the world to create an official   government-sponsored website dedicated to mapping 751 areas controlled by Sharia-ists where non-Muslim French citizens are warned to enter at their own risk. Known as No-Go Zones, these areas are called "Zones Urbaines Sensibles" translated as "Sensitive Urban Zones". Government has confirmed that some NO GO zones have devolved into lawlessness, drug dealing and gang violence.   The list in French, with both street addresses and maps, all in PDF, can be found in the appendix at JoyBrighton.com.

The boundaries in red, NO GO ZONES are neighborhoods so dangerous that even the French police services are reluctant or unwilling to enter. Sharia-ists have installed a kind of de-facto Shariah Law.

There are government confirmations or citizens reports of No Go Zones in Germany, Belgium, Netherlands and Sweden.

"The French government has announced a plan to boost policing in 15 of the most crime-ridden parts of France in an effort to reassert state control over the country's so-called "no-go" zones: Muslim-dominated neighborhoods that are largely off limits to non-Muslims."

Special acknowledgement to Daniel Pipes of the Middle East Forum for first writing about these No-Go zones in 2006.
source: danielpipes.org

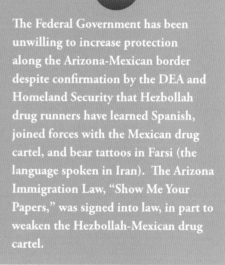

insight
box

The Federal Government has been unwilling to increase protection along the Arizona-Mexican border despite confirmation by the DEA and Homeland Security that Hezbollah drug runners have learned Spanish, joined forces with the Mexican drug cartel, and bear tattoos in Farsi (the language spoken in Iran). The Arizona Immigration Law, "Show Me Your Papers," was signed into law, in part to weaken the Hezbollah-Mexican drug cartel.

Homeland Security Reports in 2006 confirmed that Hezbollah is linked to Mexican drug cartels operating on both sides of the southern U.S. Border. In Feb. 2012, former Chief of Operations for the U.S. Drug Enforcement Agency, Michael Braun, testified before Congress that the terrorist group, Hezbollah, has developed strong, sophisticated relationships with Mexican drug cartels.

The 9/11 Commission Report has 59 references to terrorist activity in Arizona and makes reference to a classified CIA/FBI report titled "Arizona's Long-Range Nexus for Islamic Extremists."

- 20% of estimated 1.8 million Muslims in America are converts, of these 54% are women and 46% are men - 2011 Pew Research

- 49% of converts in America, converted by the age 21- 2007 Pew Research

- 58% of converts in America, converted for :religious reasons" - 2007 Pew Research

- 18% of converts in America, converted for "family and marriage reasons" - 207 Pew Research

- 33% of converts in America , are African-Americans

- 33% of African-American inmates convert in U.S. Prison.

- 20% of new converts to Islam in America are Latino - 2013 wlrn.org

http://www.huffingtonpost.com/2013/04/29/american-female-converts-to-islam-facing-growing-scrutiny_n_3181654.html

Why Are More Latinos Converting to Radical Islam?
Dec 9, 2010 7:31 AM CST

NPR reports that Latino converts are being radicalized in the US—and al-Qaeda appears to be specifically recruiting them, because they can move around the country without suspicion. Why? One expert says "I think that it is in that intersection with prison radicalization, gang culture, religious zealotry that you have a potential problem."

newser.com, Dec. 2010.

insight box

How many of these American Converts have been converted to Islam the religion? How many are knowingly or unknowingly slowly being converted to Sharia-ism, the political movement of Radical Islam? How do we help young potential converts understand the difference and draw the line between Islam and Sharia-ism?

Breaking News: Minnesota teen-jihadis suspected in Kenyan Mall Massacre. Oct. 2013

 1 Sept 2006: Taxi drivers refuse passengers with alcohol or seeing eye dogs.

2 2006 til present: The first known American suicide bomber along with at least 20 Somalian-American teens have been "radicalized in their hometown in Minnesota" according the FBI Director Robert Meuller. Parents of these teens are stunned and fearful.

 3 Oct 2007: Taxpayer Funded Footbaths at Minneapolis Airport.

4 2008: Landmark Settlement, Gold n 'Plump meat packer sued for "religious discrimination" agrees to paid prayer breaks, exemption from handling pork and $365,000 settlement.

5 Jan 2009: Taxpayer funded Islamic charter school (TIZA), one of 13 being investigated.

6 March 2009: Minn. Housing Agency offers tax-payer subsidized Shariah mortgages.

 A 2011 Congressional Report confirmed that at least 40 young American-Somalias, (many recruited in the Twin Cities) are members of Al-Qaeda linked group and "pose a direct threat to U.S. Homeland."

"Three former young recruits, now back in America, have testified that they were talked into fighting by charismatic, devout older men who promised paradise for those who died in combat against "invaders."

Women Converts to Islam are Susceptible to Conversion to Sharia-ism
Converted wife of Boston Bomber grew up "All-American"

According to Pew Research 2011 and 2007, 54% of Americans who converted to Islam were women, and approximately 20% converted before the age of 21.

- *"Many young female converts speak of wanting to be a good Muslim and a good wife; the two become equated, acted out in a life of feminine submission, first to her husband and then, by extension, to Allah."*

  - Clarionproject.org, March 2013

Converts to Islam

T. Tsarnaev

insight box

This young woman converted to Islam the religion, not Sharia-ism. However, under the influence of her Sharia-ist husband she tolerated violent beatings and isolated herself from family and friends. She may have known of her husband's dream of Jihad, yet stayed silent, and remained in the marriage.

We must educate our young American women on the difference between Islam and Sharia-ism. Every American must learn the signs of creeping Sharia-zation, to protect those we love. Germany has launched such a campaign (Chapter 11).

Katherine Russell is the the widow of the Boston Bomber Tamerlan Tsarnaev. Born and raised in Rhode Island, the thrid daughter of physician Dr. Warren Russell and nurse Judith Russell. By 21 years old, Katherine had converted to Islam, and was married with a baby. She refused to press charges when her husband Tsarnaev was arrested for violently assaulting her in 2009.

Childhood friend said "None of us would have dreamed that she would marry so young or drop out of college and have a baby or convert or be part of any of what's happened. She's just not the same person at all.'

- Dailymail.co.uk, April 2013

 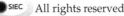

As of 2010, approximately:

"recent statistics show that 1 out of 3 African-American inmates in U.S. prisons convert to the Wahhabi type of Islam (embraced by the 9/11 highjackers) while incarcerated. The indoctrination of American inmates is a well known strategy detailed in al Qaeda training manuals."

Douglas Hagmann, Director Northeast Intelligence Network, homelandsecurityus. com archives 3503, Feb 2010

insight box

Conversion to Radical Islam or Sharia-ism gives inmates a sense of righteous power, supremacy and control in and out of prison.

For example, James Larry, 31, converted to Islam in U.S. Prison in 2007. In 2010, after his release, he confessed to killing his 19 year old pregnant wife for refusing to wear "muslim garb". He stands accused of murdering 3 other family members for not complying with his "faith".

israelnews.com

The Saudi Fifth Column On Our Nation's Campuses

By: Lee Kaplan

FrontPageMagazine.com | Monday, April 05, 2004

"Saudi money sets up these academic departments, but U.S. taxpayers underwrite the programs themselves. This is done through Title VI funding mandated by Congress. Originated in the late 1950s during the Cold War, Title VI received an additional $86 million dollars after 9/11 as part of the Education Act. This allowed the creation of 118 Middle East Resource Centers at U.S. colleges and universities. In these centers, Arabic would be taught and security analysis developed for use in the War On Terror, but the program has been seriously abused. Most Middle East Studies departments let their students slide with minimal Arabic instruction. The focus is instead on research articles that sound the anti-American and anti-Israeli drumbeat."

"Title VI money (also) goes to what could be considered the Saudis' "foot soldiers" on campus: Arab student activists."

insight box

Despite being written in 2004, this article written by Lee Kaplan remains one of the most comprehensive publications on this issue. The list of Universities defending Shariah Law continues to grow with the ongoing infusion of Mid-East Petrodollars. Examples include: Georgetown, Yale, Duke, Howard, & Syracuse.

The Saudi government spends an estimated $5 billion each year on schools, mosques and Islamic centers around the globe. These institutions often promote the Saudi government's brand of Wahhabi Islam, which supports Sharia-ism.

Books of Concern found in American Textbook Council Report:

  History Alive! The Medieval World and Beyond, by Bert Bower and Jim Lobdell

  History Alive! Teacher's Curriculum Institute; McDougal Littell

World History: McDougal Littell

Across the Centuries: Houghton Mifflin World History Book - Junior High

Connections to Today World History, Prentice Hall - High School

Modern Times: McGraw Hill, California flagship high school world history book.

The Modern World: Pearson Prentice

Modern Times: Glencoe

  The Americans: McDougal Littell

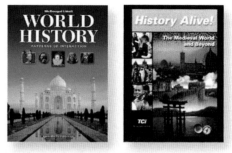

Summary Points of ATC Report:

• History textbooks present an incomplete view of Islam that misrepresents its foundations and challenges to international security.

• Misinformation about Islam is more pronounced in junior high school textbooks than in high school textbooks.

• Outright textbook errors about Islam are not the main problem; the more serious failure is the presence of disputed definitions and claims that are presented as established facts.

• Deficiencies about Islam in textbooks copyrighted before 2001 persist and in some cases have grown worse. Instead of making corrections or adjusting contested facts, publishers and editors defend misinformation and content evasions against the record. Biases persist. Silences are profound and intentional.

• Particular fault rests with the publishing corporations, boards of directors, and executives who decide what editorial policies their companies will pursue.

• Publishers have developed new world and U.S. history textbooks at three different grade levels. Errors about Islam that occurred in older textbooks have not been corrected but reiterated. Publishers have learned of contested facts and have had the time to correct imbalances. But instead of making changes, they have sustained errors or, in deliberate acts of self-censorship, have removed controversial material.

© Facebook

A Texas high school has come in for criticism from parents and a state governor after this photograph of students dressed in burqas appeared on Facebook

Parents of students at a Texas high school are outraged after discovering their children have been encouraged to dress in Islamic clothing in discussion of September 11th "freedom fighters".

According to mother of a 15 year old girl in photo, students were told that they could no longer use the terms suicide bomber or terrorist. Instead, they were instructed to use the words 'freedom fighters.'

One of the students in the burqa photo believes the teacher didn't want to teach this particular unit but had to because it was in the curriculum.

Dailymail.co.uk.

Superintendent of schools John Valastro defends curriculum, state guidelines and this specific lesson.

"What is more dangerous - fear and ignorance or education and understanding?"

"We might see it as terrorism, but from the Islamic side they might call it jihadist or freedom fighter,"

Dailymail.co.uk, huffingtonpost.com 2/13

State Sen. Dan Patrick reports that the students were forced to write an essay based on an article in The Washington Post that blamed Egypt's turmoil on democracy rather than the Muslim Brotherhood.

insight box

The "Common Core" curriculum intended to create a standard balanced quality education across America has exploded into controversy. One of many concerns is the mixing of facts and politics. Here, state educators approve a lesson which confuses religion, Islam, Sharia-ism, terrorism and women's rights.

 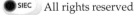

Ads denied by MTA

Denied by MTA Detroit-Michigan Oct. 2013

Denied by MTA in Washington D.C., Chicago, San Francisco, Ft. Lauderdale. July 2012.

Look carefully at the ads on the left, which have been rejected by various Mass Transit Authorities because CAIR and other Sharia-ist groups claim they are offensive.

Look at the ads to the right which have been accepted by various Mass Transit Authorities.

Ads accepted by MTA

Thanks to the legal work of the American Freedom Law Center, Mass Transit Authorities (MTA) in Miami, New York, Chicago, Washington D.C. and San Francisco are remedying their double standard and unconstitutional Free Speech Bias.

"South Park" creators Trey Parker and Matt Stone

"South Park," a popular Comedy Central cartoon series, altered its script and image depicting the prophet Muhammad in a bear costume after receiving an online threat from a radical Muslim group.

insight box

The censoring of the Mohammad cartoon by "South Park" and its parent company Viacom, whether understood or not, is a decision to obey Shariah blasphemy laws in order to avoid consequences of Shariah Islamic Law; namely death or threat fatwas. This is an example of "dhimmi(s)" submitting to Shariah Islamic Law. Corporate decisions like this set an unintended consequence of stifling constitutionally protected free speech which enables Sharia-ism in America.

 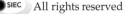

insight box

2009: Upon threats of violence, Random House stops the printing of a novel by Sherry Jones which is loosely based on the child bride of Mohammed named Aisha. **Sharia-ists** were able to bully one of the largest publishing houses in the world to give up their rights to Free Press. This is how Sharia-ism gains strength.

The Random House Publishing Group

Ballantine Books ▪ Del Rey ▪ Modern Library ▪ One World ▪ Presidio Press ▪ Random House ▪ Random House Trade Paperbacks ▪ Villard

After sending out advance editions of the novel THE JEWEL OF MEDINA, we received in response, from credible and unrelated sources, cautionary advice not only that the publication of this book might be offensive to some in the Muslim community, but also that it could incite acts of violence by a small, radical segment.

We felt an obligation to take these concerns very seriously. We consulted with security experts as well as with scholars of Islam, whom we asked to review the book and offer their assessments of potential reactions.

We stand firmly by our responsibility to support our authors and the free discussion of ideas, even those that may be construed as offensive by some. However, a publisher must weigh that responsibility against others that it also bears, and in this instance we decided, after much deliberation, to postpone publication for the safety of the author, employees of Random House, booksellers and anyone else who would be involved in distribution and sale of the novel. The author and Ballantine subsequently agreed to terminate the agreement, with the understanding that the author would be free to publish elsewhere, if she so chose.

The Random House Publishing Group

In September 2010, journalist Molly Norris announces "Everyone-Draw-Mohammad Day" to protest the silencing of free speech by Shariah blasphemy laws.

Death Fatwa is issued by Imam Anwar al-Awlaki, American convert to Islam, directed at Molly Norris.

FBI tells Molly that it cannot protect her and urges her to take threat seriously. Molly has been in hiding since September 2010 at her own expense.

THE FIRST AMENDMENT
CONGRESS SHALL MAKE NO LAW RESPECTING AN ESTABLISHMENT OF RELIGION, OR PROHIBITING THE FREE EXERCISE THEREOF; OR ABRIDGING THE FREEDOM OF SPEECH, OR OF THE PRESS; OR THE RIGHT OF THE PEOPLE PEACEABLY TO ASSEMBLE, AND TO PETITION THE GOVERNMENT FOR A REDRESS OF GRIEVANCES.

insight box

In an October 2010 article published in American Thinker, J.R. Dunn, the author of Death By Liberalism, writes that in 1988 Salman Rushdie similarly offended the Islamic world with his novel and nations and people stood as one, lining up to buy his novel in solidarity while U.K. Prime Minister, Margaret Thatcher, ordered full protection for the author.

In the case of Molly Norris, however, there was little media wide condemnation of this fatwa, few rallying citizens, few cries to protect American Political Speech, and President Obama remained "strangely silent."
What is the role of the U.S. Government in protecting its citizens?

What is Creeping *Shariah?* What tactics does it use?

1) The term "Creeping *Sharia-ism*" is used to describe the slow, deliberate, and methodical tolerance and acceptance of the Shariah way of life.

2) Sharia-ists essentially use "bullying" tactics to intimidate, shame, or threaten decision makers into accommodating their supremacy demands for special treatment.

3) There is concern that American converts to Islam are being pulled into the movement of *Sharia-ism*, knowingly or many unknowingly.

4) Read Chapter 8 to learn how American women are facing abuse, forced marriages and honor murders under creeping American *Sharia-ism*.

5) The high rate of conversion to Islam in USA, increasing home-grown sharia-ization, and the full veiling by women living in America, underscores the educational need to understand the differences between Islam and **Sharia-ism**.

This chapter lists incidents of Creeping *Shariah* in Europe and the U.S.

6) Threats of violence are compelling publishers and comedy writers to censor their material.

7) Examples of of creeping *Shariah* and the growth of *Sharia-ism* in Europe:

- As many as 750 Shariah NO GO zones too dangerous for secular police to control in France, England, Holland and Germany.
- Muslim women forced to go to Shariah Courts where rulings favor men.

8) More examples of of creeping *Sharia-ism* in America can be found in Chapter 13 of this book

- The training of Muslim chaplains in U.S. Prisons and U.S. military by American based MB groups.
- Omission of the words "Islam," **"Shariah,"** and **"Jihad"** in U.S. counter-terrorism reports.
- Unwillingness to identify and prosecute Saudi Funded Muslim Brotherhood groups, like ICNA, CAIR, ISNA and MPAC in America.
- FBI and MTA retraction of "global terrorism" bus ads, after criticism as "anti-Islam."

Chapter 10

Shariah Lawfare

Strategic Abuse of U.S. Judicial System to set Legal Precedents of Shariah Acceptance.

Major General Charles Dunlap (pictured below) coined the term "lawfare" in a 2001 essay written at Harvard University's Carr Center. His definition of lawfare is:
"...the use of law as a weapon of war," and "the strategy of using, or misusing, law as a substitute for traditional military means to achieve an operational objective."

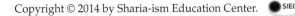

The Washington D.C. Lawfare Project describes lawfare as:
"The abuse of Western laws and judicial systems to achieve strategic military or political ends," and "...the manipulation of domestic legal systems (by state and non-state parties) to implement laws inconsistent with general principles of liberal democracy."

"Although Muslims make up less than 2 percent of the United States population, they accounted for about one-quarter of the 3,386 religious discrimination claims filed with the E.E.O.C. last year."

- S. Greenhouse, October 2010

"The Sharia-ism movement has two wings – one violent and one lawful, which can operate apart but often reinforce each other. While the violent arm attempts to silence speech by burning cars when cartoons of Mohammed are published in Denmark, the lawful arm is skillfully maneuvering within Western legal systems, both here and abroad." Brooke M. Goldstein, Family Security Matters, 2008

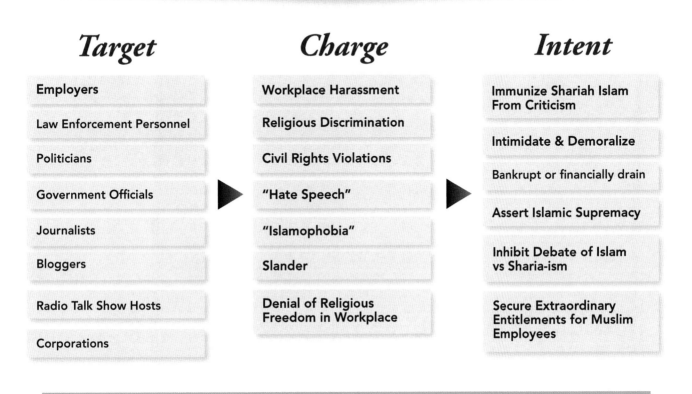

Target

- Employers
- Law Enforcement Personnel
- Politicians
- Government Officials
- Journalists
- Bloggers
- Radio Talk Show Hosts
- Corporations

Charge

- Workplace Harassment
- Religious Discrimination
- Civil Rights Violations
- "Hate Speech"
- "Islamophobia"
- Slander
- Denial of Religious Freedom in Workplace

Intent

- Immunize Shariah Islam From Criticism
- Intimidate & Demoralize
- Bankrupt or financially drain
- Assert Islamic Supremacy
- Inhibit Debate of Islam vs Sharia-ism
- Secure Extraordinary Entitlements for Muslim Employees

insight box

Shariah Lawfare targets professionals who are reporting, researching, challenging or investigating any aspect of Shariah Islam. The goal of Shariah Lawfare is to silence opposition to and debate of Shariah Islam.

"People who make statements connecting CAIR to terrorism should understand the legal consequences of their attempted slander and defamation."

- Parvez Ahmed, Chairman, CAIR

Rabiah Ahmed "has stated that lawsuits are increasingly an 'instrument' for it to use."

- Rabiah Ahmed, staff member, CAIR

insight box

If CAIR, represents the moderate voice of American Muslims as they claim, why are they discouraging American-Muslims from connecting with law enforcement? Isn't this a red flag?

Some Islamic organizations such as AIFD (American Islamic Foundation for Democracy), are thanking the NYPD for keeping New York City safe, and encourage all Americans to work with law enforcement.

CAIR

"It's very important not to speak with law enforcement of any type, not just FBI agents. We're talking about the New York Police Department; we're talking about tax agents; we're talking about everyone."

CAIR Board Member Lamis Deek
CAIR-NY Annual Banquet

"Islam isn't in America to be equal to any other faith, but to become dominant. The Koran, the Muslim book of scripture, should be the highest authority in America, and Islam the only accepted religion on earth."

Omar Ahmad, Chairman of Council of American Islamic Relations,
Speaking at conference sponsored by the Islamic Study School in Hayward
July 1998, as reported by San Ramon Valley Herald, Lisa Gardiner, July 4, 1998

 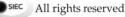

The Shariah Blasphemy Police in America ? Inventor of Islamophobia crusade?

Sample of Press Releases by CAIR from random 2 month period.
"anti-Muslim" & "Islamophobia" charges, first step in possible Shariah Lawfare.

March 2014 Press Releases

• CAIR exclusive: Documents reveal Feds may have attended Virginia anti-Muslim training
• CAIR Seeks Hate Crime Charges After Muslim Called 'Terrorist' at Calif. Costco
• CAIR Says Harassment of Md. Muslim Journalist Exposes Tenn. Mosque Opponents' Bigotry
• CAIR-San Diego Asks GOP Women's Group to Drop Anti-Muslim Speaker
• CAIR-FL, Students to Urge Embry-Riddle Univ. to Drop Anti-Muslim Event
• CAIR -Defeat Anti-Education Bill in Florida Senate Motivated by Islamophobia - CAIR - Calls on Fla.
  University to Drop Anti-Muslim Professor as Speaker.

February 2014 Press Releases

• CAIR-AZ Condemns ADL's Stereotyping of Muslims in Bill 1062 Debate
• CAIR-WA to Seek FBI Probe of Bias Incidents Targeting Mosque
• CAIR-NJ 'Disappointed' at Dismissal of Suit Against NYPD's Muslim Spying
• CAIR- Religious Freedom' Rep Funded by Same Group that Backs Islamophobes -CAIR Asks Virginia Sheriff
  to Drop Anti-Muslim Trainer
• CAIR-MD Welcomes Removal of Anti-Muslim Article from Talk Radio Website - CAIR-NJ Files Complaint for
  Firing of Muslim Woman Over Hijab

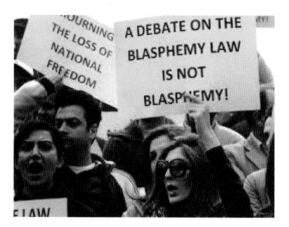

When Americans say "what Shariah Law been imposed in America?" The answer is The Shariah Blasphemy Law. Where? Any media, college, business, or government group who walks on eggshells or engages in "politically correct speak"when dealing with an issue even remotely related to religion or the Middle East or the Muslim Brotherhood or Shariah or Islam has already submitted to the most potent Shariah law, the Blasphemy Law.

The silence of political speech is essential for the survival of any totalitarian movement, including Sharia-ism.

CAIR's Vision Regarding Islamophobia in America

Our vision looks toward the time when being Muslim carries a positive connotation and Islam has an equal place among many faiths in America's pluralistic society.

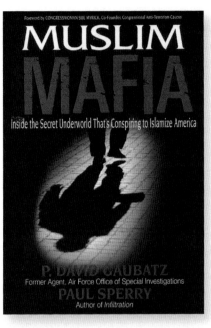

In a chapter titled "Blackmailing Corporate America," the authors show how CAIR tries to intimidate major corporations like Nike, Bank of America, and U.S. Airways, and media figures like radio talk show host Michael Savage.

Muslim Mafia is an account of a six month penetration of Washington D.C. based CAIR. Thousands of pages of documents were uncovered by Chris Gaubatz (son of author), who posed as a Muslim convert and became a CAIR intern for six months.

Author Dave Gaubatz is a counter-terrorism investigator and former federal agent with vast experience in the Middle East. Author Paul Sperry is a veteran reporter on the war on terror and author of "Infiltration," which documents CAIR's role as a U.S. front for the Muslim Brotherhood.

insight box

"CAIR is a radical voice that deliberately attempts to be seen as centrist so that media time goes to CAIR and once on the air, CAIR directs its rhetoric to the benefit of its extremist clients. CAIR is not a civil rights organization but is instead a political organization designed to advance the Shariah supremacist agenda that is directly opposed to the existence of a free society that includes respect and dignity for all people and all religions."

- Excerpt Savage vs. CAIR lawuit

Later, Washington Judge upholds right for MTA to reject similar "offensive" ad by concerned citizens

June 2013:
Under pressure from CAIR, ACLU, Congressman McDermott and Seattle Mayor who claimed "racial profiling", the FBI pulled its Washington State "Faces of Global Terrorism" bus ad (left) with photos of 16 Terrorists (most Muslim) named on the FBI's most wanted global terrorist list.

Source: komonews.org,

"You're pointing a finger at a group of people, profiling them," "I don't think that's fair and I don't think its good for our society."

—*Congressman McDermott (WA-?)*

Complaints that FBI-created Faces of Global Terrorism Ad on buses is offensive. FBI drops ad.

National Security is sacrificed and First Amendment Free Speech violated in the name of Political Correctness by MTA, the State Department and Lower Court Judge Jones of Washington State.

2013: In response to the FBI's removal of its "offensive" MTA advertisement (top blue ad) , American Freedom Defense Initiative (ADFI) created its own, similar advertisement, adding the word "Jihadis". MTA denied this red ad, despite originally accepting the government's blue ad above. Lower Court Judge Jones ruled that MTA Seattle King County decision to reject the red advertisement was "reasonable," specifically noting that displaying pictures of Muslim and Arab terrorists and labeling them "jihadis" is offensive to Muslims. The American Freedom Law Center is appealing this ruling in upper court in Jan 2014.

www.americanfreedomlawcenter.org

Similar Ad which labels terrorist as "Jihadis" is rejected by MTA. Judge says rejection is reasonable. Case going to Appeals Court.

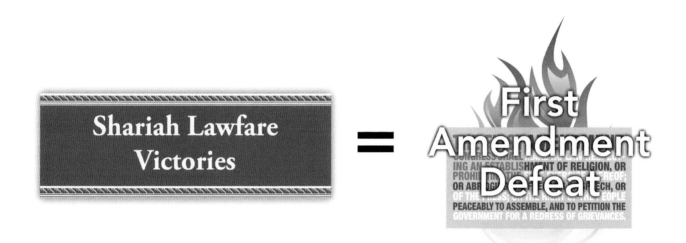

Shariah Lawfare Victories = First Amendment Defeat

Incident: Rifqa Barry converted to Christianity at 13 years of age and suffered repeated death threats and physical abuse by her Shariah faithful father, who declared that any apostate, including his daughter, must be killed. In July 2009, then 17 yr-old Rifqa fled her Ohio home to seek protective shelter with Florida friends.

Rifqa: "Well, I'm a Christian, and my parents are Muslim. And they can't know about my faith — well, they do now. But they've threatened to kill me. I don't know if you know about honor killing….You guys don't understand. Islam is very different than you guys think. They have to kill me." "You talk about religious freedom?" she asked. "No! I don't have that. I want to be here. I want to worship Jesus freely. I don't want to die. All I want is freedom of Religion. Isn't that what America is about?"

insight box

CAIR lawyers defended Rifqa's father's right to control his "unruly" daughter and sued Ohio minister Brian Williams for driving Rifqu to bus station to escape her father's death threats. Williams was charged with "contributing to the unruliness" of a minor and "interference with custody."
In 2011, the Florida Supreme Court denied the teen's religious freedom and ordered Rifqa to be returned to Ohio State's custody where she would go back to "densely populated groups of Muslims with connections to radical Islam and al-Qaeda operating in her hometown."

Incident:

Local Minneapolis Target Store: Cashiers object to handling pork products because it is banned by Shariah Islamic Law.

Outcome:

Minneapolis-based Target Corporation has offered 3 options to cashiers: 1) wear gloves, 2) shift to other positions, or 3) transfer to nearby TARGET stores.

insight box

Why the quick accommodation by Target? Why did these cashiers make this new demand from one day to the next? Why does one apply for supermarket cashier if unwilling to handle unislamic pork or beer?

How will this precedent affect U.S. employment law? When does "reasonable" become "unreasonable" in a secular society?

In 2006, Cambridge University Press (CUP) published Alms for Jihad: Charity and Terrorism in the Islamic World, by authors J. Millard Burr and Robert O. Collins.

Saudi businessman, Sheikh Khalid Bin Mahfouz, initiated a libel suit in the UK against Cambridge Press, because the Alms for Jihad book identified him as a source of terror financing.

In 2007 Cambridge Press chose to settle this libel case in which they 1) issued a comprehensive apology, 2) paid substantial damages, and 3) pulped unsold copies of the book.

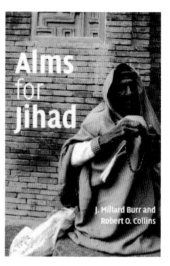

J. Millard Burr and
Robert O. Collins

insight box

The publisher of Alms for Jihad, recalled all books on store shelves and burned the inventory. This is a stark example of the extent to which the threat of violence and ruinously expensive litigation are effective in stifling the publication of a fully researched and documented book which connects Islamic tithing to Jihad funding.

Case

Halla Banafa filed a claim with the EEOC after she was turned down at age 18 for a job stocking merchandise at an Abercrombie Kids store in Milpitas, CA, September 2010, because she refused to remove her hijab while working.

Issue

The suit alleges that A&F refused to accommodate the applicant's religious beliefs by granting an exception to its "Look Policy," an internal dress code that includes a prohibition against head coverings.

insight box

Status

As of 2012, three suits like this have been launched against Abercromie and Fitch. The company has repeatedly made this public statement "We are committed to providing equal employment opportunities to all individuals regardless of religion, race or ethnicity....We comply with the law regarding reasonable religious accommodation." Status of suits remains undisclosed.

Dress codes are important to many businesses who use clothing to support their brand and image. Clothing requirements are clearly stated in employment contracts. Is it unreasonable to ask citizens in a secular society to seek employment in establishments which have no conflict with one's religious or cultural code?

 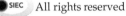

Department of Justice

Office of Public Affairs

FOR IMMEDIATE RELEASE   Monday, December 13, 2010

**Justice Department Files Religious Discrimination
Lawsuit Against Berkeley School District in Illinois**

WASHINGTON -- The Justice Department today announced it has filed a lawsuit against Berkeley School District, Berkeley, Ill., alleging that the school district violated Title VII of the Civil Rights Act of 1964 by failing to reasonably accommodate the religious practices of Safoorah Khan, a Muslim teacher at McArthur Middle School.

Issue: Illinois middle school teacher (with employment record of less than 2 years), asks for a 3 week leave of absence to take an Islamic pilgrimage known as "Hajj." The Illinois School District denies this request as an "unreasonable religious request."

This lawsuit is based on a charge of discrimination then filed by Ms. Khan with the Chicago District Office of the Equal Employment Opportunity Commission (EEOC). The EEOC referred this case to the U.S. Justice Department, which agreed that the school is discriminating against this teacher.

The U.S. Justice Department, under the leadership of Attorney General Eric Holder, then filed a lawsuit against this school district for failing to reasonably accommodate the religious practices of this teacher.

Statement by U.S. Justice Department:

This is the first lawsuit brought by the Department of Justice as a result of a pilot project designed to ensure vigorous enforcement of Title VII against state and local governmental employers by enhancing cooperation between the EEOC and the Civil Rights Division.

The filing of the lawsuit reflects the Civil Right's Divisions ongoing commitment to actively enforce federal employment discrimination laws. Additional information about the Civil Rights Division of the Department of Justice is available on its website at www.usdoj.gov/crt.

insight box

Why wasn't the religious discrimination suit by the teacher resolved in the court system, perhaps at the supreme court level? Why did Attorney General Holder feel compelled to file a lawsuit against this school?

Dec 2011: Hertz sued by Muslims employees who refuse to clock in and out during paid prayer breaks.

Hertz instituted a policy that Muslims were required to clock in and out for their PAID twice daily prayer breaks, because prayer breaks were being extended and abused.

These Muslims refused, and filed a "religious discrimination" suit. Hertz was faced with the same charges two years ago by many of the same 25 Muslims and settled "out of court." In this second lawsuit Hertz fired these employees and vows to fight this lawsuit.

Aug 2011: CAIR sues HEINZ for discrimination against Muslim workers. Heinz provided two prayer rooms "to take prayer breaks as a special accommodation to the requirements of their faith." Workers say that this special accommodation was not sufficient.

January 2012: Muslim prison inmates in Ohio file and reach settlement on lawsuit against prison for serving pork and not providing Halal beef. Ohio State argues that providing halal meals could bankrupt the state's food service system since thousands of inmates have declared themselves Muslim.

The Muslim inmates (including death row inmate Abdul Awkal) claim that vegetarian and non-pork options offered by the prison system are not good enough and that the prison system's failure to provide halal meals is a restraint on their religious freedoms. Judges in Ohio, Georgia, California, and Oklahoma uphold religious rights and mandate that strict Halal meals be made available in prisons.

THE
CATHOLIC UNIVERSITY
of AMERICA

December 2011: Catholic University of America is hit with a complaint by the D.C. Office of Human Rights because university failed to offer rooms for prayer that had no Catholic Religious symbols.

Shariah Lawfare Defeats = First Amendment Victory

Case

Pro-Israel group "American Freedom Defense Initiative" represented by American Freedom Law Center sues Mass Transit Authority for violating its Constitutional rights of Freedom of Speech and Press.

Issue

The MTA refused to run an anti-jihad advertisement that, according to the MTA, referred to Israel's enemies as savages who engaged in jihad. The MTA claimed that it violated the MTA's policy against displaying "images or information that demean an individual or group of individuals on account of race, color, religion, national origin, ancestry, gender, age, disability or sexual orientation."

Status

July 2012, Judge Paul A. Engelmayer of Federal District Court, ruled that the rejected ad was "not only protected speech — it is core political speech," "is afforded the highest level of protection under the First Amendment."

MTA considered this ad "demeaning" and refused to place on New York City buses

insight
box

Political speech and debate is often extreme or distasteful to some, because passions run high with "hot" topics, like this one.

However, the "hotter" the topic, the more important peaceful political free speech and debate becomes. Examples are global warming or gay marriage.

Case

Council on American-Islamic Relations (CAIR) and American Civil Liberties Union (ACLU) vs. FBI

Issue

Lawsuit alledges that FBI violated the 1st Amendment rights of hundreds of Muslims by using a paid informant to target and monitor several Southern California mosques based solely on religion.

FBI Spokeswoman Laura Eimiller wrote that "the FBI does not target houses of worship or religious groups but does focus on people who are alleged to be involved in criminal activity, regard- less their affiliations, religious or otherwise."

Status

A Federal District Court dismissed ruling that allowing the case to proceed could risk disclosure of government secrets, and violate individual rights to national security.

insight box

If houses of worship are exempt from investigation, what is to prevent their use as a cover for raqueteering networks such as sex, drug, or gun trafficking? Would you sue the FBI for pursuing trafficking concerns in your local church, synagogue or temple?

Sept 2007: Joe Kaufman, Chairman of Americans Against Hate, and Founder of CAIR-Watch, was sued by several Saudi Funded Muslim organizations for defamation and harassment. They cited an article he wrote, criticizing the sponsors of a Muslim social event, which was sponsored by the Islamic Circle of North America (ICNA) and the Islamic Association of North Texas (IANT), both Muslim Brotherhood off-shoots.

"The fear is that, if one writes something that is disagreeable to Islamist (Sharia-ist) groups – even if it's based entirely on fact, which my article was – he/she will be sued. And in my case, I was sued for writing about groups more than half of which I had never heard of. The chilling effect is real, and the intimidation is real."

— Joe Kaufman

insight
box

Legal Ruling: Dismissed. Though this suit was dismissed, the goal of this "lawfare" was achieved. Kaufman incurred significant legal expenses and loss of income. In addition, while difficult to quantify, journalists, reporters, and media outlets have chosen not to report on creeping Shariah in America for fear of suffering similar defamation lawsuits.

CASE

CAIR sued David Gaubatz, co-author of Muslim Mafia, and his son Chris Gaubatz in federal court in October 2009 for conspiracy.

ISSUE

CAIR charged that the father-and-son team conspired to conduct an undercover investigation of its operations by having Gaubatz's son work as an intern in CAIR's Maryland-Virginia office. During the internship's six-month period, the younger Gaubatz "copied some 12,000 documents and recorded CAIR meetings to prove the group's links to worldwide jihad ."

STATUS

Suit dismissed, was refiled and dismissed again, February 2010. And re-opened for a third time in 2012.

insight box — David Horowitz told WND. "...They know they can't win the case, but they can chill the First Amendment Free Speech by making it so expensive to speak against them that few will challenge Saudi-funded CAIR. In the end, they can just keep getting more and more money from overseas and burn out opposition with lawsuits."

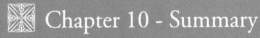

Shariah Lawfare aims to set Shariah-friendly legal precedents.

1) The goal of *Shariah* Lawfare is to set legal precedents that protect and enable the growth of *Sharia-ism* in America.

2) *Shariah* Lawfare is the in-authentic predatory use of First Amendment Freedoms of Religion, Press and Speech to legally drive a political Shariah agenda. For example, criticism of Islam (protected free speech under the First Amendment) is forbidden under *Shariah* Law. So **Sharia-ists** have taken the tactic of re-framing this criticism as illegal "hate speech". This twist of free speech is being globally endorsed by Hillary Clinton (as the former Secretary of State) and President Obama as part of a U.N. resolution 16/18.

3) The Council of American Islamic-Relations (CAIR) is the driver of *Shariah* Lawfare in America.

4) Targets of *Shariah* Lawfare often accommodate *Shariah* demands, and settle "out of court." This enables the growth of *Sharia-ism* in America.

5) Typical charges in *Shariah* Lawfare suits are: workplace harassment, religious discrimination, civil rights violation, and Islamophobia hate speech. These charges are meant to intimidate or bankrupt and inhibit debate of *Sharia-ism*.

6) *Shariah* Lawfare often targets counter-terrorism experts and journalists who are educating the public about the *Sharia-ism* threat.

Chapter 11

World Leaders Stand & Take Action Against the Sharia-ism Movement

◀ 'The West is asleep on the issue of Islamist extremism'

Former U.K. Prime Minster Tony Blair
- *Telegraph.com 2013*

▼ U.K. Prime Minister David Cameron

Prime Minister Cameron suggested there should be greater scrutiny of some Muslim groups which receive public money but do little to tackle extremism.

"Let's properly judge these organizations: Do they believe in universal human rights - including for women and people of other faiths? Do they believe in equality of all before the law? Do they believe in democracy and the right of people to elect their own government? Do they encourage integration or separatism? These are the sorts of questions we need to ask. Fail these tests and the presumption should be not to engage with organizations."

U.K. Prime Minister David Cameron
- *February 2011*

67

Chancellor Angela Merkel said Muslims must obey the constitution and not Shariah Islamic Law if they want to live in Germany, which is debating the integration of its 4 million-strong Muslim population.

"Now we obviously have Muslims in Germany. But it is important in regard to Islam that the values represented by Islam must correspond with our constitution. What applies here is the constitution, not Shariah Islamic Law."

- German Chancellor Angela Merkel, Oct 6, 2010

VERMISST

Das ist unser Sohn Tim. Wir vermissen ihn, denn wir erkennen ihn nicht mehr. Er zieht sich immer mehr zurück und wird jeden Tag radikaler. Wir haben Angst ihn ganz zu verlieren – an religiöse Fanatiker und Terrorgruppen. Wenn es Ihnen so geht wie uns, wenden Sie sich an die Beratungsstelle Radikalisierung unter 0911 – 943 43 43 oder beratung@bamf.bund.de
Mehr Informationen finden Sie auf www.bamf.de/beratungsstelle

▲ German Original

"The purpose of this campaign is to mitigate the threat of home-grown terrorist attacks...a move that reflects mounting concern in Germany over the growing assertiveness of Salafist Muslims, who openly state that they want to establish Islamic Sharia law in the country and across Europe."
source: Gatestone Institute

(Translation)
MISSING

"**This is our son, Tim.** We miss him, because we don't recognize him anymore. Day by day he is becoming distant and more radical. We are afraid of totally losing him to the hands of fanatics and terrorist organizations. If you have the same concerns as us, contact the Radicalization Consultancy Center hotline by calling 0911-9434343 or sending an email to beratung@bamf.bund.de."

insight box

The hope of this campaign, featuring a fictional German friend, brother, and son, is to encourage family members, friends, relatives, and teachers to come forward about friends or relatives who have recently become radicalized. According to the 2012 report *Radicalization Processes in the Context of Islamic Extremism and Terrorism*, German agencies estimate that approximately 1,140 individuals living in Germany pose a high risk of becoming Islamic terrorists. The report also states that up to 100,000 native Germans have converted to Islam in recent years, and that "intelligence analysis has found that converts are especially susceptible to radicalization".
This campaign remains active in Germany as of Dec 2013 and is posted in primarily in high immigrant areas. Ironically, some groups say this campaign is "racist".

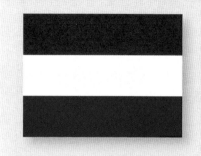

The Dutch government says it will abandon the long-standing model of multiculturalism that has encouraged Muslim immigrants to create a parallel society within the Netherlands. In a 15 point plan, the government will introduce new legislation that outlaws forced marriages, mandates that immigrants understand Dutch Law, and ban burqas and niqab (face veil) in schools and public venues.

insight box

According to a *Maurice de Hond* poll published by the newspaper *Trouw* on June 19, 2012 seventy four percent of Dutch voters said immigrants should conform to Dutch values. Moreover, eighty three percent of those polled support a ban on burqas in public spaces.

Dutch Minister Donner presented the Integration Bill to Parliament which reads:

"The government shares the social dissatisfaction over the multicultural society model and plans to shift priority to the values of the Dutch people. In the new integration system, the values of the Dutch society play a central role. With this change, the government steps away from the model of a multicultural society."

Q: Is the policy of encouraging the religious and cultural differences of immigrants not working?

Q: *"My answer is clearly yes, it is not working."*

"We have been too concerned about the identity of the person who was arriving and not enough about the identity of the country that was receiving him."

"The French national community cannot accept a change in its lifestyle, equality between men and women and freedom for little girls to go to school."

"If you come to France, you accept to melt into a single community, which is the national community, and if you do not want to accept that, you cannot be welcome in France."

- French President Sarkozy, TV debate. 2011

"Equality under the law is a core value of British justice. My bill seeks to preserve that standard. My bill seeks to stop parallel legal, or 'quasi-legal,' systems taking root in our nation. Cases of criminal law and family law are matters reserved for our English courts alone."

"Through these proposals, I want to make it perfectly clear in the law that discrimination against women shall not be allowed within arbitration. I am deeply concerned about the treatment of Muslim women by Shariah Courts. We must do all that we can to make sure they are free from any coercion, intimidation or unfairness. Many women say, 'we came to this country to escape these practices only to find the situation is worse here'."

- *Baroness Cox proposes bill to protect equality and women from Shariah civil rights abuses. June 7, 2011*

"No society can function effectively with a parallel quasi-legal system, with some people having, in practice, drastically diminished legal rights because of their religion and their gender."

- *Baroness Cox, Sept 2012*

insight box

2012 reports that British-Muslim women are being threatened for not covering themselves with a burqa and prosecution of two Imams alleged to have arranged two child marriages (girls 11 & 13) has greatly increased public support for this bill.

Jim Fitzpatrick
MP of Poplar and Canning Town; an area with a population dominated by Bangladeshi Muslims.

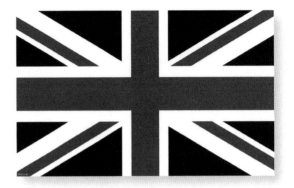

"I'm concerned that they (Shariah Courts in UK) are creating a cultural stranglehold over their communities and leading to Islamification of our society."

"Shariah courts are utterly opposed to equal rights and they discriminate against women"

- Jim Fitzpatrick, MP, 2011 Chair of Debate

One Law for All co-spokespersons Maryam Namazie and Anne Marie Waters spoke against Shariah Islamic Law in Britain and called for an end to its practice under the Arbitration Act of 1996.

2012-2013 British bill seeks to dismantle Shariah Courts and criminalize rulings. BBC undercover video confirms abuse of women.

" the Arbitration and Mediation Services Bill is now pending in the UK parliament, which seeks to put an end to Sharia tribunals, especially in England and Wales. Continuing to operate as a legitimate court could result in criminal penalties. "

-November 2012. christiannews.net

U.K. Shariah rulings reported by 2009 Civitas study:

1. No Muslim woman may marry a non-Muslim unless he converts to Islam. Until then, she loses custody of her children.

2. Woman has duty to have sex with her husband on demand.

3. Divorce is unilaterally denied despite wife or child abuse by father.

insight box

Must watch this heartbreaking 2013 BBC undercover video of U.K. Shariah "Councils" in Leyton, U.K. Muslim women dare not go to British Courts , because they risk severe punishment   by husbands.

BBC Panorama: *the Reality of Shariah Courts in the U.K.*

International Campaign Against Shari'a Court in Canada

"We oppose the current two-tier legal system of secular and religious courts; where religious tribunals make binding rulings on family legal matters based on formal and informal religious laws, codes and values.

We, the undersigned collectively believe in a secular court and 'one law for all,' and recommend that all family legal matters be removed from the Arbitration Act of Ontario, 1991. We also believe that all family legal matters should be administered by a secular Family Court, subject to the Family Law Act of Ontario."

Canadian Council of Muslim Women Le conseil canadien des femmes musul-masnes

The National Association of Women and the Law, the Canadian Council of Muslim Women, and the National Organization of Immigrant and Visible Minority Women of Canada argued that under Shariah Islamic Law, men and women are not treated equally.

National Association of Women and the Law

National Organization Of Immigrant And Visible Minority Women Of Canada

NOIVMWC

Promoting Canadian women's equality through action, legal research and education.

insight box

Premier Dalton McGuinty announced that Ontario will reject the use of Shariah Islamic Law and will move to prohibit all religious-based tribunals to settle family disputes such as divorce.

His announcement came weeks after hundreds of demonstrators around the world protested a proposal to let Ontario residents use Islamic law for settling family disputes. To the left are statements by supporting groups.

 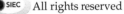

An illuminated minaret in Zurich. New ones are banned.

The New York Times

GENEVA — In a vote that displayed a widespread anxiety about Islam and undermined the country's reputation for religious tolerance, the Swiss on Sunday overwhelmingly imposed a national ban on the construction of minarets, the prayer towers of mosques, in a referendum drawn up by the far right and opposed by the government.

The referendum, which passed with a clear majority of 57.5 percent of the voters and in 22 of Switzerland's 26 cantons, was a victory for the right. The vote against was 42.5 percent. Because the ban gained a majority of votes and passed in a majority of the cantons, it will be added to the Constitution.

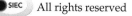

The Prime Minister of Turkey, Tayyip Erdogan, considered by many Turks to be an Islamic fundamentalist stated: "The mosques are our barracks, the domes our helmets, the minarets our bayonets, and the faithful our soldiers."
A minaret is a tower equipped with speakers from which the Call To Prayer is announced, usually five times a day.

insight box

France Soir Photo

"Street prayers must stop because they hurt the feelings of many of our compatriots who are shocked by the occupation of the public space for a religious practice," said French Interior Minister Claude Gueant.

Police could be asked to arrest Muslims who continue to pray in the street, Mr. Gueant warned. Officials will, however, initially try to persuade them to move into a mosque.

insight box

A survey by Ifop, for the France-Soir newspaper, shows that nearly 40% of French voters believe Muslim prayer in the streets of France resembles an occupation.

More than 4 city blocks have been blocked off for prayer, eliminating access to shops, cars, taxis and metros.

"An approval would be paradoxical since it is a crime in Saudi Arabia to establish Christian communities," and since Saudi Arabia is "not open for religious freedom."

Norwegian foreign minister, Jonas Gahr Stør

The Islamic Center of Tawfiq is seeking approval to use foreign funds to finance its new mosque. The Norwegian foreign minister, Jonas Gahr Støre says no mosques will be built in Norway with funding from the Saudi Government or Saudi individuals because it would be "paradoxical and unnatural if it was given approval for funding from sources in a country which is not open for religious freedom."

JNAS GAHR STØRE

178

Germany:

Nearly half of forced marriage brides in Germany are German citizens. These girls are often married overseas in Muslim-majority countries, and return home with a husband who is a family relative, entitled to German Citizenship.

British authorities fear that hundreds of teenage girls traveling from the UK during the school holidays risk being forced into family-arranged marriages, The Karma Nirvana Charity says putting a metal spoon in underwear has saved young girls. British airport personnel are trained to recognize a spoon as a signal for help

spoon

—*The Times of India, Fox News 2013*

Great Britain:

The National Center for Social Research estimated 5000 - 8000 forced marriages in U.K as of 2012. A 2012 survey of 1400+ reported forced marriages in the U.K. found 33% of victims to be minors- school children. 97% of girls were reported to be "Asian", a politically correct euphemism for "Muslim" used in Europe.

The Dept of Children, Schools & families, and U.K. Forced Marriage Unit.

No Federal Law & only 9 State Laws against Forced Marriage in USA despite 3,000 cases in 2010-2011

While Hindu & Sikh & Indians also practice forced marriage; the overwhelming majority of forced marriages practiced in "Western" countries is Islamic. Some Muslims import their cultural "non-American" practices into America. Most Hindu, Sikh and Indians abandon conflicting cultural practices when they come to America.

insight box

179

May 2012:

Shaykh Amer Jamil says forced marriage has no place in Islam and has **launched a groundbreaking campaign against forced marriage in Scotland, with the cooperation of the Government.**

During the next few weeks leaflets and sermons are being given in mosques as part of an initiative to educate the community.

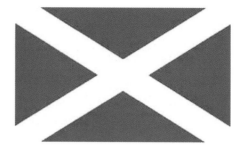

"In the Muslim community there's a misconception amongst some people that religion allows this (forced marriage), that parents have an Islamic right to choose partner of their children, and that they don't have a choice in this. "

- *Shaykh Amer Jamil*

"Every year hundreds of young people are at risk of being taken abroad, by their parents and forced to marry against their will."

"The majority of cases involve families from South Asia, particularly Pakistan, India and Bangladesh. The overwhelming majority of these families are Muslim."

"Forced marriages can involve kidnapping, beatings and rape"

- www.bbc.co.uk

insight box

A July 2010 poll conducted by the ***Pew Global Attitudes Project*** shows widespread support in Europe for banning Islamic veils in public (including schools, hospitals, and government offices). The survey shows that 82% of French, 71% of Germans, 62% of Britons, and 59% of Spaniards support such a ban. One of the earliest signs of Shariah control is the veiling of women.

Germany (2011): Hesse becomes the first German region to ban the burqa.

France (Sept 2010): Act of parliament bans wearing of face-covering headgear including niqabs and burqu.

Belgium (April 2010): Belgium's lower house of parliament votes for a law that would ban women from wearing the full Islamic face veil (burqa) in public.

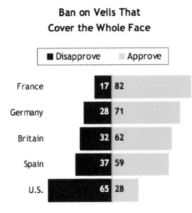

Ban on Veils That Cover the Whole Face

	■ Disapprove	Approve
France	17	82
Germany	28	71
Britain	32	62
Spain	37	59
U.S.	65	28

Pew Research Center Q59 & Q59fra.

Niqab & Burqa

Hijab

Niqab (face veil) & Burqa not permitted.   *Hijab permitted*

"The Burqa is sensory, deprivation and isolation chamber. It is moveable prison. One's ability to speak, hear, and be heard is compromised, as is one's peripheral vision, sense of smell & ability to eat or shop in public. Some women have described wearing a burqa as the equivalent of being buried alive."

Dr. Phyliss Chesler is a women's rights leader, author, psychotherapist, and Islamic Gender Apartheid expert.

Italy: (2011) Ban passes parliamentary Commission. "Final approval will put an end to the suffering of many women who are often forced to wear the burqa or niqab, which annihilates their dignity"

- Barbara Saltamartini, VP Freedom People Party

Sweden: (2011) Teachers free to ban Islamic veils. "Classroom lectures are an interplay between people, and ..., such interactions require that you can see each others' faces."

- Education minister Jan Björklund

Quebec: This ban "is a matter of deep principle that goes to the heart of our identity and our values of openness & equality."

- Jason Kenney, Minister of Citizenship & Immigration.

Swiss Region: Just banned in late 2013.

Advocacy group for Canadian Muslims, The Muslim Canadian Congress calls for wider ban, saying burqa and niqab are "symbols of gender inequality and Islamic extremism".

-Farzana Khan, former president of Muslim Canadian Congress, Toronto Sun, Jan 22, 2012.

(Jaime Vargas/IowaWatch illustration)

Hassen Chalgoumi, the Imam of Drancy—known for his outreach to Christians and Jews—announced he is in favor of a ban on the niqab: "A man who knows nothing about religion and sees a woman hidden from head to toe, what is he going to understand from that religion?" he asked. "The burqa is a sign of extremism, and it's normal that the state is fighting against that."
A few days later a "commando" of 80 men burst into Chalgouni's mosque and threatened to get rid of "the imam of the Jews."
NYTimes.com 2010

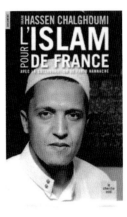

Thhe France-Soir daily published the chilling testimony of a young woman who was nudged and pushed by her husband from hijab to jilbeb to niqab to total seclusion. The couple's devout Muslim families and neighbors looked on with approval as the young woman disappeared behind the veil, hiding her despair and the bruises inflicted by her violent spouse. One day she turned for help to Ni Putes Ni Soumises, threw off her veil, divorced, and began to live again. But she is terrified that "they" will find her and kill her

❖ Psychoanalyst Fethi Benslama exposes the "masochism" of the self-imposed veil, "unacceptable even in the name of individual freedom."

❖ Poet and scholar Abdelwahab Meddeb calls the niqab the "ideological sign of radical Islam."

❖ Fadela Amara, undersecretary for Urban Affairs and former president of Ni Putes Ni Soumises [Neither Whores Nor Doormats] calls the niqab "the visible, physical expression of fundamentalists."

insight box

Information on this page sourced from Wall Street Journal online article by Nidra Poller "No Niqab Chez Nous."

November 5, 2013:

According to police, two female teens dressed in all black and wearing burqas approached the woman and asked if they could use her cell phone.

The expectant mother said no, and that she would place the call for them. That's when the girls, between the ages of 13 and 15, knocked the woman to the ground and tried to rob her before fleeing.

- frontpagemag.com

insight box

Countries who have banned the Burqa cite reasons of women inequality and marker of Islamic Extremism.

In addition, countries who have banned the burqa cite its security risk. A victim (i.e. kidnapped child) will be difficult to identify and rescue, and a criminal (i.e. kidnapper) will be difficult to identify and capture. The Burqa heightens the personal and national security risks of all people.

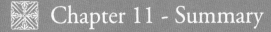

World Leaders say multi-culturalism has created a conflicting parallel society which de-values women and fosters extremism and radicalization of vulnerable youth.

1) British Prime Minister Cameron, former Prime Minister of Spain Aznar, German Chancellor Merkel, French President Sarkozy, and Dutch Minister Donner have publicly stated one or all of these statements:

- Multiculturalism has created parallel societies and fosters extremism
- *Shariah* Islamic Law is incompatible with their country law.

2) A marker of growing *sharia-ization* across Europe is the appearance of fully veiled Muslim women. In response, France, Belgium, Germany, Italy, Sweden, Quebec and Swiss Region have banned the *burqa* and *niqab* (face veils). Lawmakers say face veil violates equal rights of women, which is protected under their country law.

3) Alarming rates of *Sharia-zation* among German youth, has prompted the government to launch a Radicalization Consultancy Center and hotline to help families assist in intervention. Self declared "moderate muslim" groups in Germany have denounced this campaign as discriminatory.

4) 2013: The British Justice Department reversed their earlier acceptance of *Shariah* Courts and is trying to dismantle over 150 *Shariah* Tribunals whose rulings discriminate against women and are contrary to U.K. Law. *Shariah* judges refuse to cooperate.

 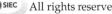

Europe bans burqa & face veil as marker of women inequality & Sharia-ism.

5) Muslim groups in Quebec successfully lobbied to ban *Shariah* Courts in 2005.

6) Great Britain considers legislative action to ban *Shariah* Law.

7) 2009: Switzerland bans the building of minarets. A mineret is a tall, slender tower equipped with amplification to publicly call Muslims to prayer. It is often connected to a mosque.

8) European airport security is on the alert for young girls (citizens) with European passports and citizenry who are "visiting family" in Islamic countries. There is a serious pattern of these girls being married overseas and returning with husbands entitled to dual citizenship based on marriage. A U.K. child welfare charity, Karma Nirvana, suggested that girls put a spoon in their underwear which will set off airport scanners and alert security.

9) Austria, Belgium, Cyprus, Denmark, Germany, Malta, Norway Pass Laws to Criminalize forced marriage. U.K., Sweden, Switzerland & Greece set to follow in 2013.

10) 2010: Norway bans the construction of mosques which are funded by Saudi Arabia.

Chapter 12

**A Small Sample of Muslim, Hindu and Sikh
Leaders Stand Against the Sharia-ism Movement**

The Sharia Conundrum

Watch Hasan Mahmud's latest movie about the uses and abuses of Sharia Law. Enjoy!

www.hasanmahmud.com

"A dream of millions materialized by common villagers! They eliminated radicalism in their 28 villages ONLY with knowledge. No money. No muscle. No media. No political blessing. This shows how simply one book and one movie can be powerful tools of social change, through a peaceful process. Muslims Facing Tomorrow offers this to the Muslim world."

—Hasan Mahmud, 2014

Canadian Hasan Mahmud spent 15 years writing a book in his native Bangladeshi which documents that Sharia Law is not sanctioned by the Quo'ran. Then he produced The Sharia Conundrum video (left) which tells the story of a family being torn apart as they begin to live under Sharia rule. Ten books (below) and one video were given to 3 villages, who then passed these on. In one year, 28 Bangladeshi villages have declared they are Zamat (radical) Free Village. Go to hasanmahmud.com to watch this video. Then watch sensational video responses from"enlightened" Bangladeshi men & women.

Raheel Raza is President of The Council for Muslims Facing Tomorrow & author of book: Their Jihad – Not My Jihad. She speaks about Honor Violence in 2014 Honor Diaries film.

Hand-made signboard proudly posted on a tree at the entrance of the village Bagerhaat in southern Bangladesh.

Sharia, Undoing the Wrongdoing Book by H. Mahmud

 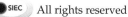

"Shariah is a derogatory and backward concept which denies human rights to women. It is an antithesis of freedom and democracy...Shariah is incompatible with our Constitution."

Narain Kataria, President
Indian American Intellectuals Forum

insight box

On Sept 7, 2011, the Indian American Intellectuals Forum issued a press release titled: Appeal to Save Hindus and Sikhs from Extinction in Pakistan to World Leaders, the U.N., President Obama and Global Human Rights Groups. This press release details the forced conversion of men to Islam under threat of losing their jobs, the forced conversions of young girls, choice of conversion to Islam or payment of 12 million rupees Dhimmi "Jizya tax" by Sihks, public announcements of death to anyone who violates Shariah Blashemy Law & mass kidnappings. Narain Kataria fears that the last safe haven in the world (USA) will no longer be secure as *Sharia-ism* slowly takes hold in America.

 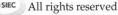

"We Muslims in Canada defeated an attempt by Islamists to sneak Shariah Islamic Law into Ontario."... "We recognized the damage Shariah had inflicted on Muslims in the UK, and its oppressive nature in Muslim-majority countries, and decided to oppose it. We urge American Muslims not to succumb to the Islamists propaganda, and to back the Michigan Bill, which will protect Muslims and non-Muslims alike from the impact of foreign laws that violate the U.S. or Michigan constitutions."

- Tarek Fatah

Tarek Fatah is a Canadian writer and broadcaster as well as a passionate, secular, Muslim libertarian activist. He is the founder of the Muslim Canadian Congress. Fatah advocates gay rights, a separation of religion and state, opposition to Shariah Islamic Law, and advocacy for a "liberal, progressive form" of Islam. Mr. Fatah wrote *Chasing a Mirage: The Tragic Illusion of an Islamic State* (2008), and *The Jew Is Not My Enemy: Unveiling the Myths that Fuel Muslim Anti-Semitism* (2010).

insight box

Tarek Fatah urges American Muslims to remember the oppression that fellow Muslims live under in many of their native countries and to support a law which protects their constitutional freedoms known, which is known as Michigan Laws for Michigan Courts. As of June 2012, Representatives Walch and Bolger, Senator Richardville, and Hamas-CAIR were the last blockade to passing this bill. The bill has 80% popular support (according to a May 2012, CBS News poll). The proposed Michigan ALAC bill was defeated in 2013. It is expected to be reintroduced soon.

Manda Ervin held offices in several Iranian Government ministries in Iran prior to the overthrow of the Shah by Ayatollah Khomeini. After the revolution, she fled Iran and founded The Alliance of Iranian Women. She educates western governments and the media along with human rights and women's organizations on the threat of Shariah Islamic Law and the plight of Muslim women and children.

"Shariah Islamic Law, wherever it has been applied in the public domain, be it in Iran, Saudi Arabia or Pakistan, has resulted in untold misery and oppression of Muslims, in particular Muslim women, by Islamists and dictators who invoke Shariah Islamic Law to justify their rule."

 "Many of us fled the Muslim world to escape Shariah Islamic Law and to practice Islam in our personal lives, by moving to the USA and other western countries. We do not wish these laws to follow us here."

- Manda Ervin

"We want to be Americans. Religion is a private issue. We ran away from 'political Islam' in Iran, but it has followed us.... CAIR [the Council on American-Islamic Relations] has created this image that all 3 million Muslims in America are the same and CAIR represents them — which is not true."

- Manda Ervin, 2010, Capital Hill hearing, Congressional Anti-Terrorism Caucus, Washington D.C.

FORMER MUSLIMS UNITED

Amil Imani

writer and critic of Islam

Wafa Sultan

Author of book:
A God Who Hates

Nonie Darwish

Author of Book: Now They Call
Me Infidel ; Cruel and Unusual
Punishment

Ibn Warraq

Author of book:
Why I am not a Muslim

insight box

Former Muslim United (FMU), a group of American apostates and renowned authors, live in America under the imminent threat of death fatwas because they converted away from Islam. FMU asked 165 American Muslim Leaders to sign a Freedom Pledge that grants freedom from persecution to all apostates. Only two leaders signed this pledge. No Muslim community or Islamic Center came out in support of this pledge. See next page for details.

FORMER MUSLIMS UNITED

The Freedom Pledge by FMU

To support the civil rights of former Muslims, also known as apostates from Islam, I sign "The Muslim Pledge for Religious Freedom and Safety from Harm for Former Muslims":

I renounce, repudiate and oppose any physical intimidation, or worldly and corporal punishment, of apostates from Islam, in whatever way that punishment may be determined or carried out by myself or any other Muslim including the family of the apostate, community, Mosque leaders, Shariah court or judge, and Muslim government or regime.

insight box

Dr. Zudhi Jasser, Founder of the American Islamic Center for Democracy, and Ali Aylami, Executive Director of Democracy and Human Rights, were the only two American Muslim Leaders (of 165), who signed this Freedom Pledge. Both men live with death threats.

Ali Aylami   **Dr. Zuhdi Jasser**

Muslim Leaders speak out against CAIR and *Sharia-ism*

1) Distinguished Indian American, Sikh, Apostate, Women's Rights, and Civil Libertarian Muslim Leaders call on American leaders to recognize the threat to First Amendment Freedoms posed by the acceptance of *Shariah Islamic Law* in America.

2) Former Muslims United group of apostates living in America asked 165 Muslim leaders to sign "Freedom Pledge." Only two of the American 165 Muslim leaders signed this pledge. Under *Shariah Islamic Law* the penalty for becoming an apostate is death.

3) It is hard to believe that American Presidents Clinton, Bush Sr., Bush Jr. and Obama have all embraced Sharia-ist and Muslim Brotherhood groups at White House State dinners and events, while ignoring the authentic Muslim leaders. The acceptance of Muslim Brotherhood influence in the U.S. Government runs deep. So deep that a 2012 request by 5 Congressman to investigate these influences was denied by the U.S. House Intelligence Committee, pre-empting debate on the House and Senate floor.
See page 192

Chapter 13

Failures of U.S. Leaders to Address the Threat of Sharia-ism

1

Governor Patrick and Mayor Menino ignore warnings since 2002 of the radical Islamic Society of Boston Cultural Center and Mosque, where the Tsarnaev Boston Marathon bombers attended.
Here's what they knew:
thanks to 10 years of unheeded warnings by Boston Watchdog group, Americans for Peace and Tolerance.

Dzhokhar Tsarnaev   Tamerlan Tsarnaev

- The Islamic Society of Boston (ISB) organization was founded by A. Ala-moudi who today serves a 23-year prison sentence for raising money for al-Qaeda. The 70,000 square ft. ISB Cultural Center (mosque) was complete in 2009. Half of the $15 million budget was Saudi funded.

- FBI documents report that Imam of ISB-Roxbury campus, partnered directly with American born convert to Islam Anwar Awlaki . Awlaki became leader of Al-Qaeda, and was assassinated in 2011 U.S. drone attack. Awlaki urged American Muslims to attack crowded sporting events and published article in Al-Qaeda magazine describing how to make pressure cooker bombs.

- The ISB Mosque is operated by Muslim American Society (MAS) , identified by federal prosecutors as American front for the Muslim Brotherhood group.

- IRS records show original trustee of ISB Mosque to be Sheikh Qawadari, a religious cleric banned from entering UK and USA for his connections to terror. Qaradawi says Islam will "conquer America" and "conquer Europe", and urges Muslims to kill homosexuals and Jews on YouTube.

- The ISB mosque's website contained instructions on how to beat one's wife.

Charles Jacobs, Founder of Americans for Peace and Tolerance

2 **President Obama continues to endorse Muslim Brotherhood President Morsi after Egyptians mounted a civil revolution to oust the Muslim Brotherhood. President Obama refuses to acknowledge that the Muslim Brotherhood is the leader of global Sharia-ism.**

"we are deeply concerned by the decision of the Egyptian Armed Forces to remove President Morsi and suspend the Egyptian constitution. I now call on the Egyptian military to move quickly and responsibly to return full authority back to a democratically elected civilian government as soon as possible through an inclusive and transparent process, and to avoid any arbitrary arrests of President Morsi and his supporters."

- **Statement by President Obama, npr.org, July 2013**

3 Since 2002, numerous sources report that 20 - 30% of American prison inmates are urged or forced to convert to Radical Islam every year. This is more than 20 times the national average of American conversion to Islam. Yet the U.S. Government continues to employ Muslim Brotherhood groups to train and certify Muslim Prison Chaplains.

"This program is funded by Saudi Arabian money through the National Islamic Prison Foundation, which underwrites an American "prison outreach" program designed to convert large numbers of African-American inmates not only to Wahhabism, but to its political objectives — including virulent anti-Americanism."

- Cal Thomas, Washington Times, 2002, Clarion Project 2013, marksilverberg.com

 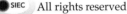

1 In an effort to calm attacks on U.S. Embassies in Eygpt (Benghazi) and Libya, the U.S. Embassy in Cairo releases an apology which "condemns the continuing efforts of misguided individuals to hurt the feelings of Muslims". (See below). In doing so, President Obama chooses not to protect U.S. First Amendment Free Speech but rather to respect Shariah Blasphemy law, which calls for the death of those who criticize the Shariah Manifesto.

U.S. Embassy Condemns Religious Incitement

September 11, 2012

The Embassy of the United States in Cairo condemns the continuing efforts by misguided individuals to hurt the religious feelings of Muslims - as we condemn efforts to offend believers of all religions. Today, the 11th anniversary of the September 11, 2001 terrorist attacks on the United States, Americans are honoring our patriots and those who serve our nation as the fitting response to the enemies of democracy. Respect for religious beliefs is a cornerstone of American democracy. We firmly reject the actions by those who abuse the universal right of free speech to hurt the religious beliefs of others.

- Official press release by Embassy of United States in Cairo

Around the timing of this Press Release Apology, a mob of Sharia-ists went onto murder U.S. Ambassador Stevens and kill 4 others in what was actually a coordinated attack of Egyptian and Libyan Embassies by al-Qaeda-like groups. It took the Obama Administration 16 days to acknowledge that this attack was not a spontaneous grass roots protest of an "anti-Islam" video.

"Somebody exercised
some terrible judgment"
- *CBS.com Jan 24*

"TO LEARN WHO
RULES OVER YOU,
SIMPLY FIND OUT
WHO YOU ARE NOT
ALLOWED TO
CRITICIZE"

-VOLTAIRE.

2 Jan 2012 - Mayor Bloomberg apologizes and shuts down the showing of the educational documentary film "The Third Jihad," to NYPD Police & Anti-Terrorism Force, in response to protest by CAIR who called the film "islamophobic". Bloomberg admits he had not seen the film.

▶ Soon after NYPD Chief Ray Kelly apologized for his endorsement of the film, after "encouragement" by the Bloomberg administration. He resigned in Dec. 2013.

The Third Jihad, named an "anti-Muslim" film by the New York Daily News, and called an "anti-Islam" film by the New York Times is narrated by Dr. Zuhdi Jasser, founder of a coalition of 25 pro-Western, liberty minded, American Muslim groups. The film is a series of interviews with former FBI, CIA, and Homeland Security officials, psych-warfare experts, former Mayor Rudy Guiliani and NYPD Counter-Terrorism Commissioner Ray Kelly. In the film, these interviewees describe how sharia-ists are establishing a worldwide regime. Ironically, one segment of the film focuses on exactly how CAIR groups are effective in silencing and eventually co-opting U.S. Officials and lawmakers.

▶ On Sept. 25, 2011, 60 Minutes lauded Ray Kelly in a feature program stating: "Ray Kelly built an organization of 50,000 personnel- more officers than the FBI- dedicated to protecting the nations biggest terrorist target." Under Ray Kelly's leadership, at least 30 terror plots across America were thwarted.

New York Police and Counter-terrorism Commission Ray Kelly forced to resign?

3 **Homeland Security whitewashes threat of Sharia-ism. Homeland Security Lexicon Report labels "Islamic Terrorists" as "military extremists". The terms "jihad", "Muslim" and "Islamic" are not identified, acknowledged or even mentioned in this lexicon report.**

4 The Obama Administration chooses to partner with Shariah-driven OIC to criminalize "hate speech", which includes criticism of Islam. This violates the U.S. Constitution in which criticism of religion is protected free speech.

"I consider it part of my responsibility as President of the United States to fight against negative stereotypes of Islam wherever they appear".

- President Obama, 2009 Cairo Speech.

OIC

The Obama administration, with Secretary of State Clinton at the helm, has decided to launch a major international effort against Islamophobia in partnership with the Saudi-based OIC (Organization of Islamic Conference).

The White House is supporting U.N. Resolution 16/18 (created in 2011). The purpose of this resolution is to criminalize "hate speech" against Islam. This is a clear U.S. endorsement of a global Shariah Blasphemy Law which punishes those who criticize Islam in any way. .

Under pressure from Sharia-ist groups, Western Europe now has laws against religious hate speech that serve as proxies for Islamic blasphemy codes.

— *Nina Shea is director of the Hudson Institute's Center for Religious Freedom and co-author, with Paul Marshall, of Silenced: How Apostasy and Blasphemy Codes are Choking Freedoms Worldwide (Oxford University Press, November 2011).*

5 U.S. Attorney General Eric Holder has not *responded* to a formal Congressional recommendation in May 2012 that the U.S. Dept of Justice sever ties with Council of Islamic Relations (CAIR).

The Fiscal Year 2013 Commerce, Justice, Science Appropriations Bill sponsored by Virginia Congressman Frank Wolf, passed the House in May 2012 . It contained a recommendation that Attorney General Eric Holder follow in the FBI's footsteps and sever ties with CAIR. Congressmen Sue Myrick, Pete Hoekstra, John Shadegg, Paul Broun and Trent Franks were instrumental in passing this bill.

The Senate is in a stalemate on this recommendation despite leadership by Senator Jon Kyl.

U.S. Attorney General Eric Holder

6 FBI continues to appease Muslim Brotherhood groups despite landmark Obama law, H.R. 2112, which bans FBI from engaging with Muslim Brotherhood groups identified as "unindicted co-conspirators" in the terror-financing Holy Land Foundation Charity Trial. For example, in February 2012, under pressure from CAIR and ISNA, the FBI purged 700 documents and 300 presentations of offensive language such as "jihad", "Shariah", or "Islam".

7 Year-long investigation by Investigative Project on Terrorism (IPT) finds that dozens of known Sharia-ists met with Obama White House officials by invitation. There has been no response by U.S. Govt.

 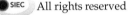

8 **Hillary Clinton, Secretary of State, Excludes Israel from International Counter-terrorism Forum (June 2012)**
Obama administration and congressional sources confirmed to Adam Kredo of theWashington Free Beacon that Israel was deliberately excluded from the forum founded by the U.S. in order to appease Arab countries that are openly hostile to Israel's very existence. **- Patrick Poole**

"the world is sliding backwards"
Source: c-span.org . Remark made by then U.S. Secretary of State Hillary Clinton to the ban on Burqa and face veil installed by France and Belgium.

9 **Hillary Clinton, Secretary of State defended a U.S. Report on Religious Freedom condemning the ban on Burqa's and Niqab by Belgium and France as an "infringement on religious freedom."** She went on say "the world is sliding backwards". **- C-SPAN.org, July 30,2012**

10 **House Minority Leader Nancy Pelosi headlined a Democratic Party fundraiser with 10 leaders of Muslim Brotherhood front groups. Executive Director Nihad Awad of CAIR, designated by the U.S. TSY as a funder of Hamas played a key role in organizing this event.**

Congresswoman
Nancy Pelosi

The invitation-only fundraiser was sponsored by Reps. Keith Ellison, D-Minn.; Andre Carson, D-Ind.; and Steve Israel, D-N.Y., chairman of the Democratic Congressional Campaign Committee. This democratic fundraiser was held at the W Hotel in Washington D.C. on May 16.

Source: investigativeproject.org

Congressman
Steve Israel (D-NY)

11 **On May 22, 2010, Massachusetts Assistant Attorney General Healy hand–to-hand accepted a $50,000 check from Imam Faaruuq of the Islamic Society of Boston (ISB) Cultural Center and Mosque, given in appreciation of the newly completed Massachusetts Islamic Sensitivity Law Enforcement Training Program.**

For 18 months prior to their Boston Marathon Jihad, the Tsarnaev brothers associated with this same Islamic Society of Boston Cultural Center and Mosque.

Three years later, Boston Law Officials are caught off guard when these same brothers kill 4 and injure 264 Americans? No one is talking about their ISB affiliation? Or the check?

Massachusetts Attorney General
Martha Coakley

Even more disturbing facts:

Attorney General Coakly developed this sensitivity course by partnering with the MAS-Muslim American Society, which is a self-reported Muslim Brotherhood created group.

The Imam of the ISB center and mosque is the radical Imam Siraj Wahhaj who is known for his anti-American rhetoric. Here is a third example in this book:

"Whoever is at war with my friends, I declare war on them...
Your true friend is Allah, the messenger, and those who believe. Americans and Canadians. Hear it well...The Americans are not your friends, hear what I'm telling you, hear it well. The Canadians are not your friends...The Europeans are not your friends...These people will never be satisfied with you until you follow their religion. "
Imam Siraj Wahhaj 1991,
frontpagemag.com, Jan 2005

Boston Marathon Bombing:
4 dead, 260 injured, 17 lost limbs

Krystle Campbell, died.

Adrianne Haslet, a professional ballroom dancer lost her leg.

Martin Richard, 8 year old, died.

CAIR

Mayor Bloomberg

12

2012 - Present

▶

Mayor Bloomberg appoints lawyer Omar Mohammedi, the General Counsel to CAIR-NY, to a position on New York City's Human Rights Commission for his expertise in employment discrimination. Mohammedi is a vocal critic of the NYPD, and has called for the resignation of Police Chief Ray Kelly for religious discrimination and for the NYPD's surveillance of mosques. Mohammedi is not a paid appointee.

13

2009 - Present

▶

Mayor Bloomberg's education policy advisor, Fatima Ashraf (also known as Fatima Shama) hosted the May 2009 CAIR-NY annual banquet and fundraiser, where she called CAIR-NY "a shining star among Muslim organizations in the country," adding that "their sincerity and motivation" and "genuine desire to make positive change for Muslims is what really makes them stand out." Fatima Ashraf-Shama is a salaried NYC employee.

insight box

Is it legal or ethical for Mayor Bloomberg to appoint leaders of New York Council of Islamic Relations (CAIR) to his administration when the FBI has been banned from engaging with this Muslim Brotherhood front group since Nov 11, 2011 under H.R. 2112 signed by President Obama?

Why isn't the CAIR affiliation of these appointees disclosed on the official New York City government Website?

14 **In June 2012, Five Congressmen wrote the letter below, calling for an investigation of the Muslim Brotherhood and its possible infiltration and influence on U.S. Government agencies.** The House Intelligence Committee summarily DISMISSED this inquiry.

The letter from these Congressmen states, "... information has come to light that raises serious questions about the involvement of organizations and individuals with the Muslim Brotherhood. Given that the U.S. G overnment has established in federal court that the Muslim Brotherhood's mission in the United States is 'destroying the Western Civilization from within' - a practice the Brothers call 'civilization jihad' - we believe that the apparent involvement of those with such ties raises serious concerns that warrant your urgent attention."

Reps Bachmann (R-Mn), Franks (R-Az), Gohmert (R-Fl), Rooney, and Westmoreland (R-Ga). referred to as "National Security Five".

National Security Five are scolded:

"Given our access to sensitive information, I also believe members of the Intelligence Committee have a special responsibility to exercise caution in making statements about national security concerns, the only reasonable action for the authors of these letters to take would be to withdraw their requests."

- Rep. Jim Langevin (D-R.I.)

insight box

Where is the public outcry when a Congressional Intelligence Committee refuses to gather information on a possible national security threat?

Michele Bachmann (R-Minn.)

Louie Gohmert (R-Texas)

Thomas Rooney (R-Fla.)

Lynn Westmoreland (R-Ga.)

"To Collaborate in this administration's political correctness and pretend that these issues are not real is to potentially put innocent lives at risk in the pursuit of preventing anyone from feeling uncomfortable"

Trent Franks (R-Ariz.)

Patrick Poole, National Security and Terrorism Correspondent, identified and described many these U.S. Government Failures in his article: Obama's National Security, 'Not Top 10,' of 2011, published by PJ Media.

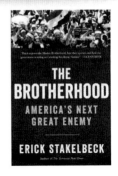

1 **Feb 2011: Director of National Intelligence James Clapper tells Congress that the Muslim Brotherhood is a "largely secular" group which denounced violence and al-Qaeda.**
Clapper was reading verbatim from a set of written briefing notes that had been prepared by the top intelligence analysts in the intelligence community.

"Muslim Brotherhood" … is an umbrella term for a variety of movements; in the case of Egypt, a very heterogeneous group, largely secular, which has eschewed violence and has decried al-Qaeda as a perversion of Islam. … They have pursued social ends, a betterment of the political order in Egypt, et cetera. … In other countries, there are also chapters or franchises of the Muslim Brotherhood, but there is no overarching agenda, particularly in pursuit of violence, at least internationally."

This statement is contrary to volumes of expert testimony regarding the Muslim Brotherhood.

- Patrick Poole, PJ Media, Dec 31, 2011

2 **May 2011: Osama bin Laden buried by U.S. military in accordance with Islamic traditions according to National Security Advisor John Brennan and funded by U.S. Taxpayers**

 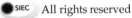

3 **July 2011:** Prominent Muslim-American Capitol Hill lobbyist, Syed Ghulam Nabi Fai, is arrested and admits he has been working as a Pakistani intelligence spy and active in American MB groups ISNA and MSA since 1985.

4 **March - Present:** Obama backs overthrow of Gaddafi, installs al-Qaeda-friendly, Shariah-compliant regime in Libya.

Despite ongoing announcements that Libya will be installing Shariah Islamic Law, President Obama on Oct 23, hailed the declaration of liberation in Libya as the "beginning of a new era of promise," urging the country to start a reconciliation process, according to a White House statement. *- Patrick Poole, PJ Media, Dec 31, 2011*

5 **Oct 2011:** White House blocks appointment of American-Muslim leader Dr. Zuhdi Jasser to State Department post after receiving top security clearance in 15 month vetting process.

Dr. Zudhi Jasser is a practicing physician and founder of the American Islamic Forum for Democracy (AIFD) and American Islamic Leadership Coalition (AILC). Senator Jon Kyl commented on the affair by saying that "the Obama administration has chosen to sideline Dr. Jasser", who is a strong critic of the Muslim Brotherhood.
- Patrick Poole, PJ Media, Dec 31, 2011

6 Seven New York State representatives claim the CIA-NYPD is "spying on Muslims" with its undercover surveillance of mosques based on NYPD and CIA intelligence. Senators Parker, Montgomery, Perkins, Rivera Huntly and representatives Liz Krueger and Ruth Hassell-Thompson asked that this "spying" be investigated.

Dr. Zuhdi Jasser

These Elected officials are unwilling to educate themselves about the difference between Mosques and Shariah Command Bases. They are blinded by the "Freedom of Religion" defense.
- Patrick Poole, PJ Media, Dec 31, 2011

1 **Neither NYC Mayor Bloomberg nor New York Governor Cuomo agreed to slow approval process or investigate alleged radical ties & mid-east petrodollar funding of "Ground Zero Mosque" promoters.** Instead, the Cordoba-Park 51 Mosque & Islamic Center, to be built two blocks from Ground Zero is strongly supported by Mayor Bloomberg, with little comment by Governor Cuomo.

Debra Burlingame

- **51% of New Yorkers "do not want this mosque built anywhere". Quinnipiac University Poll**

- **71% of Americans say "building a mosque so close to 9-11 site is inappropriate." CBS news poll.**

"We don't like being lectured about "tolerance" by the politicians & cultural elites who are in absolute denial about Shariah, and in denial about the highjackers on Sept 11th, who want to bring Shariah to America"

Ms. Burlingame is the founder of 911Families.org . Her brother, Charles F. Burlingame III, was the pilot of American Airlines flight 77, which was hijacked and crashed at the Pentagon on 9/11.

Fox News Interview, Aug 2010.

"U.S. policies were an accessory to the crime (on 9-11)."

Ground Zero Mosque Imam Rauf, CBS "60 Minutes", Oct 2011.

"We may not always agree with every one of our neighbors. That's life. But we also recognize that part of being a New Yorker is living with your neighbors in mutual respect and tolerance. It was exactly that spirit of openness and acceptance that was attacked on 9/11, 2001."

Mayor Bloomberg. Aug 2010.

Patrick Poole, National Security and Terrorism Correspondent, identified and described these U.S. Government failures in his article: ***2010: The Year of the Islamist Infiltration,*** published by PJMedia on Dec 30, 2010.

2 **May 2010: White House bans use of terms "Jihad," "al-Qaeda," "Hamas," "Hezbollah," "Caliph," "Islam," and "Shariah" in all national security documents.** The word "jihad" was invoked 126 times and Islam cited 322 times in the 9/11 Commission's report. However on this date the U.S. Govt announced that the terms "Jihad," "al-Qaeda," "Hamas," "Hezbollah," "Caliph," "Islam," and "Shariah" must be purged from all recent national security documents. This was at the request of Muslim Brotherhood-backed groups who claim that such terms legitimize terrorism.

3 **October 2010: DHS Secretary Janet Napolitano swears in Shariah-ist Mohamed Elibiary to serve as only Muslim member of the Homeland Security Advisory Council.** Elibiary has billed himself as a "deradicalization expert," despite abundant evidence of his previous defense of terrorist support organizations, his praise for jihadist authors, and his threats made against a Dallas journalist who repeatedly exposed his extremist views. - **Patrick Poole, 2010: The Year of the Islamist Infiltration**

4 **August 2010: Taxpayer funded U.S. State Department paid for Ground Zero Mosque Imam's tour of Middle East despite his extremist statements and widespread public opposition. Story uncovered by award winning investigative reporter Claudia Rossett.**
Emails from New York City Mayor Bloomberg's office show coordination between the Ground Zero mosque developers and Bloomberg staffers, including drafting statements for mosque officials and pledges to "give political cover" to the Landmarks Preservation Commission officials who gave the green light to the Mosque permit..

Claudia Rossett, an investigative reporter is recognized for her reporting on 1990 Tiananmen Square, 1994 North Korea Labor Camps, 2005 fraudulent U.N. for Food program, and 2010 Ground Zero Mosque taxpayer mis-appropriation. She is currently a journalist-in-residence with the Foundation for Defense of Democracies

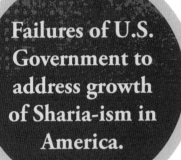

Failures of U.S. Government to address growth of Sharia-ism in America.

This Chapter highlights failures of the U.S. government to respond to the threat of *Sharia-ism*. Worse, it highlights how the U.S. government is enabling *Sharia-ism* in America, and weakening First Amendment Rights of every citizen.

While the author's decision to include each of these topics as a "U.S. Failure" is subjective, the facts of the incidents or issues highlighted are true.

Special thanks to Patrick Poole. Much of this chapter is a re-publication of his well researched 3 articles, the "Top 10" Failures of the U.S. Government in 2010 and 2011 and regarding America's national Security policies.

 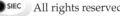

Chapter 14

U.S. Representatives & Governors Take Action: Congressional Hearings & New State Laws.

U.S. Congressmen address Sharia-ism Threat.

In the first four hearings

"King's committee.., focused on the problem of radicalization in U.S. prisons, investigated Al-Shabaab's recruitment of more than 40 young American Muslims, and examined the threat to military communities inside the U.S. following attacks at Fort Hood, Texas and Little Rock, Arkansas."

- *Examiner.com, June 19, 2012*

"When I began this series of investigative hearings in March of last year to examine radicalization within the Muslim-American community, I was vilified by the politically correct media, pandering politicians and radical groups such as CAIR – even though this issue was non-partisan and of serious concern to national security and counterterrorism officials in the Obama administration,

Congressman Peter King, Opening Remarks Fifth Hearing, June 2012

Abdirizak Bihi, a Somali American from Minnesota, described how a nephew turned radical and left to fight with an Islamic militia in Somalia. He said religious leaders had discouraged him from going to the authorities, warning that "you will have eternal fire and hell" for betraying Islam.

*Abdirizak Bihi
June 2012 testimony*

insight box

Congressman Peter King, Chairman of the House of Representatives Committee on Homeland Security has been condemned by the media and fellow U.S. Congressmen, and CAIR for doing his job gathering information to ascertain just how Secure our Homeland is.

U.S. Congressmen Voice Opposition to King Hearings on Basis of Religious Discrimination.

"It has already been classified as a way to demonize and castigate a whole broad base of human beings," said Rep. Sheila Jackson Lee (D-Tex.) She waved a copy of the Constitution and said the hearing might be a violation of laws prohibiting religious discrimination:

"Let me make it clear today that I remain convinced that these hearings must go forward, and they will. To back down would be a craven surrender to political correctness and an abdication of what I believe to be the main responsibility of this committee– to protect America from a terrorist attack."

- Congressman King, Opening Remarks First Hearing March 2011

"I do agree that we should deal with radicalization and violent radicalization, but that singling out one community is the wrong thing to do."
Congressman Keith Ellison, March 2011

insight box

U.S. Congressmen must agree to educate themselves on the difference between Islam the religion and Sharia-ism the political movement. Sharia-ism is a threat to very American citizen regardless of faith, race, sex or culture. Sharia-ism is an anti-Muslim, sexist, racist, homophobic and misogynist political movement.

Radicalized Tennessee college student murders Army Private outside Arkansas recruiting office.

Proud black American family sends their son, Carlos Blesdoe, to Tennessee State University. Proud white American family admires their son, Andy Long, who joins the 90+ year tradition of family military service.

Carlos is radicalized by Shariah Imam in college, changes his name to Abdulhakim Mujahid Muhamad ,trains in Yemen, returns home and kills uniformed Private Andy Long, and wounds Private Ezeagwula outside army recruiting office in Little Rock. June 2009.

Muhamad (Carlos) is serving life in prison.

"We must stop these extremist invaders from raping the minds" of our children. " Tomorrow it could be your son or daughter."

Melvin Blesdoe (dad) testimony at Congressional radicalization hearings in 2011. Photo of son, Carlos-Muhamed, before and after radicalization above.

This "Jihad in American has been down-played by the federal government and mainstream media..as well as flat out lying to the American people... in advancement of a political agenda over offending anyone." "The White House released a statement on Little Rock shootings, but only to Arkansas news outlets, and only if they asked for one."
Had U.S. Military been de-briefed on this attack," the shooting of 13 U.S. soldiers by Ft. Hood Jihadist Major Nidal, just four months later (Nov.2009) may have been avoided. "

Darin Long (dad) testimony at Joint House-Senate Homeland Security Committee c-span video. Dec. 2011
Photo of murdered son Private Long

Grieving fathers tell their story *Losing Our Sons* in documentary film which exposes radicalization of U.S. youth and Government white-washing of Islamic extremism. If you can help these fathers with distribution, please contact creator of this film : APT-Americans for Peace and Tolerance.

THE MOSQUE IN MORGANTOWN

A film by Brittany Huckabee

When Muslim writer and activist Asra Nomani returns to her hometown mosque in West Virginia, she believes she sees signs of trouble: exclusion of women, intolerance toward non-believers, suspicion of the West. Her resulting campaign for change alienates would-be allies in the mosque, leading many to wonder who most deserves the label of "extremist." It isn't long before members put forward a petition to expel her from the Islamic Center of Morgantown.

As Asra takes an increasingly different path from the community's moderates – marching on the mosque, posting a manifesto on its door, storming out of a community meeting and challenging a visiting sheik about domestic violence – the film provides a rare look at the real controversies that divide a Muslim community.

"The Muslim community's response to the hearings on radicalization within our community – much like the response of many communities to internal problems – hasn't been one of taking ownership of our problems, but rather engaging in a strategy of deflection. This strategy has expressed itself in our wider response to radicalization, terrorism, and the presence of an intolerant interpretation of Islam in our world today."

Asra Nomani, Washington Post, April 2013.

Asra Q. Nomani

Asra Nomani is an Indian-American journalist and activist is involved in the Muslim reform and Islamic feminist movements. She teaches journalism at Georgetown University. She is the author of *"An American Woman's Struggle for the Soul Of Islam"*.

"There were many reasons why, when called to do so, I testified in the investigative hearings held by the House Committee on Homeland Security examining radicalization within the Muslim American community."

"Islamist radicalization is ongoing in our civilian, military and prison community, as repeated findings from the investigative hearings (King) have uncovered. Unfortunately, where there should be uproar and carefully targeted actions in response to these critically important findings, we remain mired in political correctness by refusing to identify our enemies' driving ideology. Islamists (Sharia-ists) distract the discussion from the root of the problem by focusing our attention on what they call "Islamophobia.""

Dr. Qanta Ahmed

"The 2010 Quadrennial Homeland Security Review never mentions "Islamist" or "Islamic terrorism" in 108 pages. This is in keeping with President Obama's vision, which, according to then Homeland Security Assistant Secretary for Policy David Heyman, "made it clear as we are looking at counterterrorism that our principal focus is al Qaeda and global violent extremism, and that is the terminology and language that has been articulated" by President Obama and his advisers."

"Attorney General Eric Holder demonstrated this pandering in his May 2010 testimony before the House Judiciary Committee, when he attempted to discuss failed Times Square bomber Faisal Shahzad's potential motives, while avoiding the term "radical Islam." Holder's agonizing dance around the issue demonstrates just how difficult it has become to talk about the ideology fueling so many terror plots, now that the highest levels of government have banned any discussion of the role of radical religious interpretation."

Dr. Qanta Ahmed, Huffington Post. July 2012

Dr. Qanta Ahmed, honored American physician, feminist, and activist is author of "In the Land of Invisible Women," a personal memoir of working as a physician in Saudi Arabia. She was named a 2010 Templeton-Cambridge Journalism Fellow, and 2010 Power Woman by NY Moves Magazine.

U.S. State Governors Protect Citizen Rights &
Sign new Laws to Reduce Sharia-ism Threat

The story of this **FREE SPEECH Act** starts with Dr. Rachel Ehrenfeld , the director of the American Center for Democracy, who bravely stood up to a Saudi billionaire, Khalid bin Mahfouz who she connected to the funding of terror groups in her book, *Funding Evil: How Terrorism is Financed–and How to Stop It.*

Billionaire Mahfouz sued 45 publishers and journalists for "slander" and "dirtying his reputation" through the British Court (rather than U.S. Court), which didn't require him to provide much proof. All 45 targets, settled out of court. Dr. Rachel Ehrenfeld fought back against "Libel Tourism" and won.

Libel Tourism: Tactic of "shopping" for a foreign court that allows individuals to sue for defamation much more easily than they could sue in a U.S. court.

Libel tourism was being used to silence Americans from speaking out against radical Islam and other critical national security issues .

- *Front Page Magazine*, Ruth King, September 2010

insight box

In 2008, New York State Governor Paterson signed the Libel Terrorism Protection Act, known as Rachel's Law sponsored by Assemblyman Rory Lancman and State Senator Dean Skelos.   As of Sept 2013, Ilinois, Florida, California, Tennessee, Maryland, Utah. and Lousiana. have passed their own versions of Rachel's Law.

In August 2010, President Obama signed the Federal Version of Rachel's Law called 2010 Free Speech Protection Act.

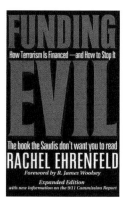

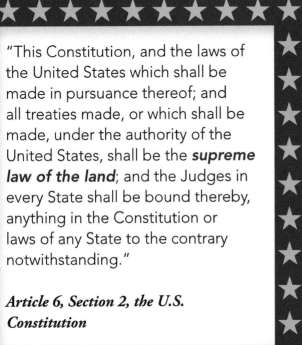

"This Constitution, and the laws of the United States which shall be made in pursuance thereof; and all treaties made, or which shall be made, under the authority of the United States, shall be the **supreme law of the land**; and the Judges in every State shall be bound thereby, anything in the Constitution or laws of any State to the contrary notwithstanding."

Article 6, Section 2, the U.S. Constitution

insight box

Some Judges in U.S. Courts are applying Foreign Laws in lieu of U.S. Constitutional Law to respect "religious or cultural sensitivities". Ruling in this manner not only violates the supremacy clause of the U.S. Constitution, it often weakens the individual rights of the American Defendant. This is the case with Shariah Islamic Law.

Lousiana Leads Nation: Governor Jindal Signs 6 New Laws To De-rail Growing Sharia-ism Influence on Free Speech, State Courts and Charitable Gifts.

(1) ***Rachel's Law protects protects freedom of speech and press of journalists, bloggers, etc,*** from predatory slander libel-lawsuits waged thru foreign legal courts. The practice of libel-tourism was muzzling researchers & experts from writing about about terror-financing, or other national security issues due to fear of financially draining foreign lawsuits .

Louisiana Act 712 signed into Law by Governor Jindal 2010

Rachels' Law signed in:

Florida, New York, California, Illinois, Tennessee, Utah, Maryland.

Federal version of Rachel's Law, "Free Speech of 2010" signed into law by President Obama in Aug 2010.

(2) ***Lousiana Laws for Lousiana Courts (version of ALAC)*** *protects all constitutional individual rights of Americans from less protective foreign laws or courts.*

Example:
Divorce and custody cases involving American wives of foreign men must be adjudicated by U.S. family law, rather than held to Shariah Divorce or Custody Laws which favor rights of husbands or fathers and discriminate against wives or mothers.

Louisiana Act 714 signed into Law by Governor Jindal 2012

ALAC Law also in:

- Alabama
- Arizona
- Kansas
- North Carolina
- Oklahoma
- South Carolina 2014
- Tennessee

(3) ***Full Disclosure Law to help track foreign dollars gifted to Lousiana colleges,*** to reduce funding of on-campus Shariah Islam programming. Public colleges & universites must publicly disclose these gifts.

Louisiana Act 715 signed into Law by Governor Jindal 2010

Full Discolsure Foreign Gift Law signed in:

- New York
- Utah
- NJ. Introducing not signed

(4) **Louisiana RICO Act is amended to include "the material support of terrorism" as a criminal RICO offense.**
Act 116 authored by Rep. Cameron Henry amends the Louisiana Racketeering Act to apply to, among other offenses, terrorism and aiding others in terrorism. By putting the material support of terrorism under the Racketeering Act, this landmark law arms state law enforcement with a useful tool with stiffer penalties for those found to provide material support for terrorism

Lousiana Act 116 signed into law 2012.

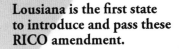 **Lousiana is the first state to introduce and pass these RICO amendment.**

(5) **Female Genital Mutilation and/or the act of removing a girl from Louisiana for the purpose of FGM is a criminal offense.**
Act 207, authored by Rep. Nancy Landry, creates the crime of: Female Genital Mutilation (FGM). The first and most infamous case of FGM actually occurred in Louisiana back in 1972

Louisiana Act 207 signed into law in 2012 by Governor Jinhal

Louisiana is first state to include the AHA Foundation model FGM language to criminalize the act of removing a girl from the state/country for the purpose of FGM.
These 19 states criminalize FGM, however the law does not protect girls taken out of state: California, Colorado, Delaware, Florida, Georgia, Illinois, Louisiana, Maryland, Minnesota, Missouri, Nevada, New York, North Dakota, Oklahoma, Oregon, Rhode Island, Tennessee, Texas, West Virginia, Wisconsin. *theahafoundation.org*

(6) **Foreign Investment Full Dislosure law protects investors from Security Fraud in Foreign Markets such as Shariah Finance.**
 Act 369 authored by Senator Danny Martiny requires full and fair disclosure when a security offered in the state of Louisiana is governed by a religious law. This landmark bill was necessitated by the increasing presence of Shariah-Compliant Finance and the almost total lack of transparency associated with such instruments.

Louisiana Act 369 signed into law in 2012 by Governor Jinhal

 Louisiana is first state to introduce and pass this Foreign Full Disclosure Law.

▶ 2010

Governor Bill Haslam of Tennessee signed "Tennessee Laws for Tennessee Courts" (modeled on ALAC) into law.

▶ 2010

Governor Jan Brewer of Arizona signed "Arizona Laws for Arizona Courts" (modeled on ALAC) into law.

▶ 2010

Governor Bobby Jindal of Louisiana signed "Louisiana Laws for Louisiana Courts" (modeled on ALAC) into law.

insight box

Despite CAIR's ongoing claims that American Laws for America Courts (ALAC) is "anti-Muslim", and "unconstitutional" , ALAC has not been challenged in law as "unconstitutional" in any of the 7 states in which it passed because the purpose of ALAC is to ensure equal protection under U.S. Law.

Joanne Bregman, citizen lobbyist and & Phylis Schlafly founder of National Eagle Forum.

These women successfully spearheaded ALAC campaign in Tennessee.

"We saw the TN Law for TN Courts bill as a legitimate vehicle to arrest the creep of Shariah into our state's jurisprudence. We know that the single issue that binds the Muslim Brotherhood, Hamas, CAIR, ISNA, ICNA and every other Islamist Muslim Brotherhood spin-off group, is the professed goal of supplanting our Constitution with Shariah Islamic Law."

- JoAnne Bregman, Tennessee Eagle Forum, 2010.

 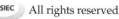

 ▶ **2012**

Governor Sam Brownback of Kansas signed "Kansas Laws for Kansas Courts" (modeled on ALAC) into law.

 ▶ **2013**

Governor Mary Fallin of Oklahoma signed "Oklahoma Laws for Oklahoma Courts" version of ALAC into law

 ▶ **2012**

South Dakota Governor Dennis Daugaard of South Dakota signs South Dakota Laws for South Dakota Courts version of ALAC

 ▶ **2013**

North Carolina Laws for North Carolina Courts version of AlAC became law by proxy without signature or veto by Governor Pat McCrory.

insight box

Alabama Laws for Alabama Courts versions of ALAC was passed by both houses in late 2013 and is awaiting signature from Governor Robert Bentley. In 2014, state versions of ALAC are being debated in Florida, Georgia, Idaho, Indiana, Missouri & Vermont, and likely elsewhere. If you are a citizen or lawyer in one of these states, and want to help educate decision makers, please contact www.publicpolicyalliance.org .

Why American Laws for American Courts (ALAC)?

America has unique values of liberty which do not exist in foreign legal systems; this is particularly true in regard to Shariah Islamic Law. Included among them, but not limited to the following, are these values and rights:

- ❖ **Freedom of Religion**
- ❖ **Freedom of Speech**
- ❖ **Freedom of the Press**
- ❖ **Due Process**
- ❖ **Right to Privacy**
- ❖ **Right to Keep and Bear Arms**

Civil and Criminal law serve as the bedrock and manifestation of American values - We are a nation of laws. Unfortunately and increasingly, foreign laws and legal doctrines, including Shariah Islamic Law principles, are finding their way into U.S. court cases.

The goal of the **American Laws for American Courts Act** is a clear and unequivocal application of what should be the goal of all state courts: No U.S. citizen or resident should be denied the liberties, rights, and privileges guaranteed in our constitutional republic. American Laws for American Courts is needed especially to protect women and children, identified by international human rights organizations as the primary victims of discriminatory foreign laws.

 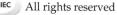

What is ALAC? Law protects U.S. Constitutional Rights when Challenged by Foreign Law.

✦ "American Laws for American Courts," known as ALAC, is part of a growing movement in America that is committed to upholding the supremacy of the U.S. Constitution in the face of any challenge by foreign law at the state court level.

✦ ALAC is a neutral law. It is designed to protect the U.S. Constitutional rights of Americans against any foreign law from any country which challenges their rights. No one single foreign law is singled out in ALAC. Globalization and the internet has made foreign travel, ex-pat residence, and multi-country business deals much more common. U.S. Judges and juries in lower courts are just starting to recognize and understand the difficulty and importance of reconciling foreign law with U.S. Constitutional law.

CLE Course on American Laws for American Courts

Source:
Law Offices of David Yerushalmi, P.C.

insight box

U.S. Judges have applied foreign Shariah Law in child custody and family law cases, rather than U.S. Law, out of misplaced respect for culture, religion or ignorance. The result: American-Muslim women and children are faced with very limited rights.
For this reason, ALAC has been passed in seven U.S. states, and being considered in dozens more. The wording of American Laws for American Courts (ALAC) is not country, culture, religion or ethnic specific. ALAC is not country or ethnic specific. For example , these words are not included in ALAC: "China," "Muslim," or "Islam."

MODEL LEGISLATION

AN ACT to protect rights and privileges granted under the United States or [State] Constitution.

BE IT ENACTED BY THE [GENERAL ASSEMBLY/LEGISLATURE] OF THE STATE OF [_____]:

The [general assembly/legislature] finds that it shall be the public policy of this state to protect its citizens from the application of foreign laws when the application of a foreign law will result in the violation of a right guaranteed by the constitution of this state or of the United States, including but not limited to due process, freedom of religion, speech, or press, and any right of privacy or marriage as specifically defined by the constitution of this state.

The [general assembly/state legislature] fully recognizes the right to contract freely under the laws of this state, and also recognizes that this right may be reasonably and rationally circumscribed pursuant to the state's interest to protect and promote rights and privileges granted under the United States or [State] Constitution, including but not limited to due process, freedom of religion, speech, or press, and any right of privacy or marriage as specifically defined by the constitution of this state.

http://publicpolicyalliance.org

This is a portion of the model text of American Laws for American Courts. Individual states may need to customize this language to conform to unique state constitutions.

The Federalist Society
for Law and Public Policy Studies

A policy study and review by Karen Lugo, of 70+ Muslim divorce cases tried in American courts (states: DE, FL, KY, LA, Mass, MD, MI, NC, NH, OH, TN, TX, VA, WA) documented that.

Findings: 25 rulings upheld Shariah terms in either the trial or appellate court, 25 rulings rejected Shariah and 20 rulings were unclear. . On appeal, more were overturned to assert American legal standards than to impose Shariah.

Shariah Islamic Law is often upheld in a U.S. Court because Islamic marriages are conducted in a Shariah court or mosque, and never licensed with the state. U.S. Family Law cases without protection of ALAC risk: systematic loss of maternal custody of children older than 9 years, legalization of polgamy, unfair financial settlement for wife, or insufficient due process.

Karen J. Lugo. American Family Law and Shariah-compliant Marriages, Published by The Federal Society for Law and Public Policy Studies. Vol. 13, Issue 2. July 2012

Karen J.Lugo, specializes in U.S.Consitutional Law. Founder of LIbertas-West Project. Co-Director of the Center for Constitutional Jurisprudence. Adjunct Clinical Professor Chapman University Law. By Request, Karen submitted a brief to the Conseil d'Etat on the legal grounds for banning the burqa in France.

insight box

Next page describes Shariah-based Marriage Practices. France, Greece & Norway has passed legislature to deny Shariah family law adjudication. Germany is expected to do the same.

 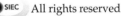

Because U.S. Judges are accepting Shariah defenses: In 2010, N.J. Judge denies protection of Muslim wife against charged marital rape. Court dismissed her rape charge against husband saying: "court believes his (husband) desire to have sex when he wanted it, is consistent with his practices and is not prohibited."

Case

Plaintiff S.D. (wife) and defendant M.J.R.(husband), Muslim citizens of Morocco, wed in an arranged marriage in July 2008, when plaintiff was 17 years old. In August 2008, they moved to New Jersey. Wife describes a continual pattern of abuse culminating on January 2009, when the defendant forced the plaintiff to have sex with him while she cried. The neighbors heard her cries and called police.

2010: Shariah "Cultural Religious" Defense.

Lower Court Ruling:
"This court does not feel that, under the circumstances, that this defendant had a criminal desire to or intent to sexually assault or to sexually contact the plaintiff when he did. The court believes that he was operating under his belief that it is, as the husband, his desire to have sex when and whether he wanted to, was something that was consistent with his practices and it was something that was not prohibited."

Shariah Defense

S.D. v. M.J.R.: Man rapes wife and claims Shariah as a defense saying "this is according to our religion, you are my wife, I (can) do anything to you. The woman, she should submit and ask her anything I ask her to do". Decided July 23, 2010.

insight box

While this is only one case, this sets a dangerous precedent that under certain foreign laws, in this case Shariah Law, marital rape is not a crime.

If ALAC were law in New Jersey at this time, this husband would be charged with the crime of marital rape, and sentenced to jail. Instead, the lower court in NJ allowed this husband who repeatedly raped his wife to walk free and this young Muslim woman living in America was denied her due process rights. This is a perfect test case for ALAC.

Fortunately, women's rights activists came to the rescue of this young woman and pro-bono representation appealed this case. The lower ruling was over-ruled.

 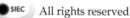

insight box

The lack of juries, pre-trial discovery, cross-examining of witnesses, and standards of paternal custody (without regard for the welfare of the child) violates the Constitutional freedoms of all Americans. It particularly discriminates against American Muslim women and children.

Shariah courts

have judges but no juries, no pre-trial discovery, and no cross examination of witnesses. Conversely, a man's testimony is given twice the weight of a woman's testimony (a woman bringing a rape charge must have four witnesses to act in court) with no focus on due process (a Muslim husband can divorce his wife simply by repeating three times he does so in the presence of an imam without notifying his wife). There is no minimum age required for a Shariah Marriage.

In child custody

disputes where the standard applied in US state courts is in "the best interests of the child," full faith and credit has been given to Islamic court decisions where a prejudicial standard exists in favor of Muslim fathers. Thus, even when an allegation of abuse by a father may be applicable, US courts would uphold an Islamic court's judgment. Should an allegation include sexual abuse, demonstrative forensic evidence would not even be allowed by Islamic courts—nor would any written evidence, such as a diary acknowledging the act, be admissible.

Non-ALAC States Risk Denial Of:

- Divorce rights
- Child custody rights
- Property rights

01:30 / 11:23

American
PUBLIC POLICY ALLIANCE

1 American Laws for American Courts is not needed because it states what is already reality in state courts.
> FALSE

2 American Laws for American Courts is not needed because Shariah and other foreign laws are not in conflict with the Constitution and state public policy in the US, and no relevant cases are in our court systems.
> FALSE

3 American Laws for American Courts interferes with foreign treaties. **> FALSE**

4 American Laws for American Courts restricts the right to contract. **> FALSE**

5 This bill impacts "comity" and violates the Full Faith & Credit Clause of the US Constitution. **> FALSE**

6 American Laws for American Courts interferes with business activity and commerce and thus would adversely impact economic development in a state. **> FALSE**

7 The business exemption language used in American Laws for American Courts violates the equal protection clause of the constitution. **> FALSE**

insight box Please to go website of American Public Policy Alliance for detailed answers to these questions and more information about ALAC.

8. Provisions of American Laws for American Courts would violate the Uniform Child Custody Jurisdiction and Enforcement Act (UCCJEA). **> FALSE**

9. American Laws for American Courts could violate the federal Parental Kidnapping Prevention Act (PKPA). **> FALSE**

10. American Laws for American Courts would violate international treaties dealing with child custody; namely the Hague Convention. **> FALSE**

11. American Laws for American Courts would interfere with English Common Law. **> FALSE**

12. American Laws for American Courts would make states that enact it vulnerable to expensive law suits. **> FALSE**

13. American Laws for American Courts would interfere with Native American tribal law. **> FALSE**

14. American Laws for American Courts would interfere with Jewish law or Catholic Canon Law. **> FALSE**

15. American Laws for American Courts unfairly targets Muslims. **> FALSE**

> **insight box** — **Please go to the website of the American Public Policy Alliance for detailed answers to these questions and more information about ALAC.**

ALAC
American Laws
for American
Courts

1) Four Congressional Hearings on the radicalization of America were held thanks to the commitment to the U.S. Constitution by Senator Peter King of New York. Senator King suffers "Islamophobe slurs" by elected U.S. Representatives who are unwilling to educate themselves on the threat of *Sharia-ism* today in America.

2) Congressmen Bachman, Franks, Gohmert, Trent, and Westmorelan have become cast as the "National Security Five," calling for Hearings on the infiltration of the Muslim Brotherhood in America. Despite volumes of serious research that documents the national security threat of the MB, members of the House Intelligence Committee have harshly criticized this fact-finding request as inflammatory and irresponsible. It seems that disclosure, transparency and due diligence is not the role of this Intelligence committee.

3) Expert on terror-financing, Dr. Rachel Ehrenfeld spearheaded national movement to protect journalists, speakers, and others from being silenced by costly, predatory libel lawsuits initiated in certain foreign courts. Rachel's law to Protect Free Speech has been passed in NY and other states. The National version of this law, known as the Free Speech Protection Act passed in 2010.

4) Louisiana has passed 6 laws in 2010 - 2012 leading the way in curbing *Sharia-ists* influence in the state.

These laws include:
- Rachel's Law Free Speech
- Lousiana Laws for Louisiana Courts
- ALAC
- Transparency of Foreign Gifts
- RICO Act Amendment to Include Material Support of Terror
- Foreign Investment Full Disclosure Law.
- Female Genital Mutilation (FGM) & abduction

5) 2010 - 2013: Arizona, Kansas, Louisiana, North Carolina, Oklahoma, South Dakota & Tennessee pass state version of ALAC.

6) "American Courts for American Laws" known as ALAC is a neutral law designed to protect the Constitutional Rights of Americans when challenged by less protective foreign law in a U.S. State Court. The last two pages of this Chapter list common mis-representations of ALAC.

7) This neutral ALAC law does not cite any country, race, religion, faith or creed by name. For example, it does not specify "Christian," "Jew," "Muslim," "Islam," or "*Shariah*."

Chapter 15

Take Action and Glossary

Religion	Politics
Islam	Sharia-ism (more precise than Islamism)
Muslim	Sharia-ist (more precise than Islamist)
Mosque	Shariah Control Center
Quo'ran	Shariah Manifesto/Law
Sheikh or Imam	Shariah Sheikh or Shariah Imam
Open Face Head Scarf - Hijab.	Burqa or Face Veil with eyes only showing
Protected under First Amendment.	Not protected under First Amendment
	Shariah Enabler Sharia-ization

- Share this book with others. Help friends distinguish Islam from Sharia-ism.

- Discuss Sharia-ism openly with friends & colleagues. Active Political speech & Debate is the mechanism that has always moved America forward.

- American women: reach out to your American Muslim women neighbors. They came to this country to enjoy U.S. First Amendment freedoms. Help them protect their families from Sharia-ism.

- Women College Students: Arrange for a screening and discussion of the Honor Diaries documentary on your campus. (page 122-123)

- Tell your state and federal representatives that U.S. courts need the American Law for American Courts (ALAC) Liberty Laws to protect the individual rights of American citizens when challenged by a foreign law.

- Visit your neighborhood mosque & Imam.

- Join an inter-faith dialogue group. Ask the hard questions: Opinion of CAIR - Council of American Islamic Relations? Treatment of Apostates? Islamophobia? Paternal child custody? Reaction to Burqa? Polygamy?

- Pay attention to what your children are learning in school.

Glossary of Abbreviations for Key Muslim Brotherhood Connected Groups

CAIR - Council of American Islamic Relations, Muslim Brotherhood connected group*

HLF - Holy Land Foundation Islamic Charity

The largest Islamic charity in U.S. as of 2001. Designated in 2001 as a terrorist organization. The 2008 trial of charity leaders considered the largest terror financing prosecution in American History. HLF supported Hamas by providing Zakat charity dollars through many Zakat networks. HLF's support of Iowa floods and Oklahoma City Bombing helped mask its terror support operations.

ICNA - Islamic Council of North America, Muslim Brotherhood connected group*

ISNA - Islamic Society of North America, Muslim Brotherhood connected group*

MAS - Muslim American Society, Muslim Brotherhood connected group*

MB - Muslim Brotherhood

NAIT- National American Islamic Trust, hold leases of majority of Mosques in America. Muslim Brotherhood connected group

Named as co-conspirator to 2007 terror financing scheme to fund Hamas thru the Holy Land Foundation Islamic Charity

The Council on American-Islamic Relations (CAIR)

"The Council on American-Islamic Relations (CAIR), headquartered in Washington, is perhaps the best-known and most controversial Muslim organization in North America. CAIR presents itself as an advocate for Muslims' civil rights and the spokesman for American Muslims.

But there is another side to CAIR that has alarmed many people in positions who know. The Department of Homeland Security refuses to deal with it. President Obama signed a law in 2011, banning the FBI was engaging with all unidicted co-conspirators named as part of the Holy Land Foundation Islamic Charity terror funding scheme. Senator Charles Schumer (Democrat, New York) describes it as an organization "which we know has ties to terrorism." Senator Dick Durbin (Democrat, Illinois) observes that CAIR is "unusual in its extreme rhetoric and its associations with groups that are suspect." Steven Pomerantz, the FBI's former chief of counterterrorism, notes that "CAIR, its leaders, and its activities effectively give aid to international terrorist groups." The family of John P. O'Neill, Sr., the former FBI counterterrorism chief who perished at the World Trade Center, named CAIR in a lawsuit as having "been part of the criminal conspiracy of radical Islamic terrorism" responsible for the September 11 atrocities. Counterterrorism expert Steven Emerson calls it "a radical fundamentalist front group for Hamas." American Muslim groups also reject CAIR's claim to speak on their behalf. "Jamal Hasan of the Council for Democracy and Tolerance explains that CAIR's goal is to spread "Islamic hegemony the world over by hook or by crook." Kamal Nawash, head of Free Muslims Against Terrorism, finds that CAIR and similar groups condemn terrorism on the surface while endorsing an ideology that helps foster extremism, adding that "almost all of their members are theocratic Muslims who reject secularism and want to establish Islamic states."

source: Daniel Pipes, Sharon Chada. Middle East Quarterly 2006.

About The Author
Joy Brighton MBA

Joy Brighton is a longtime champion of women's rights. Notably, in 1998, Joy partnered with a major international charity to create one of the earliest micro-Finance programs for women in Africa, and the first financial literacy course for women in Mozambique. Concerned about the abuse of women in America, sanctioned in the name of religion, culture or shariah, Joy published this first book, released April 2014.

Sharia-ism is Here: The Battle to Control Women – and Everyone Else

Joy Brighton is a also a former Wall Street trader who today is part of an international team of experts concerned about the non-transparent risks of the Sharia Finance market, and threat to global free capital markets.

A graduate of a top business school, Joy was a fixed-income salesperson/trader for a bulge bracket investment firm, and an adjunct Professor of Securities and Investments at various colleges. Later, with a Masters in Psychological Counseling, Joy worked as an executive coach catering to investment professionals. Joy speaks with legal, policy, grass roots, and legislative leaders who are concerned about the challenge of Sharia-ism, the political movement of Radical Islam to: America's national security, civil and women's rights, First Amendment freedoms, sovereignty of U.S. Law and free capital financial markets.

TO LEARN WHO RULES
OVER YOU, SIMPLY
FIND OUT
WHO YOU ARE
NOT ALLOWED TO
CRITICIZE

-VOLTAIRE

Made in the USA
Charleston, SC
11 July 2014